MONSTERS
OF NEW YORK

D1545798

0   11557 01213   2

MONSTERS
OF NEW YORK

Mysterious Creatures in the Empire State

Bruce G. Hallenbeck

STACKPOLE
BOOKS

Indian Prairie Public Library District
401 Plainfield Road ~ Darien, IL 60561

Copyright © 2013 by Bruce G. Hallenbeck

Published by
STACKPOLE BOOKS
5067 Ritter Road
Mechanicsburg, PA 17055
www.stackpolebooks.com

Printed in the United States of America

10 9 8 7 6 5 4 3 2 1

FIRST EDITION

Cover art by Mark Radle
Cover design by Tessa J. Sweigert

Library of Congress Cataloging-in-Publication Data

Hallenbeck, Bruce G., 1952–
  Monsters of New York : mysterious creatures in the Empire State / Bruce G. Hallenbeck.
     pages cm
  Includes bibliographical references.
  ISBN 978-0-8117-1213-2 (paperback)
  1. Cryptozoology—New York (State) 2. Monsters—New York (State) 3. Animals, Mythical—New York (State) 4. New York (State)—Social life and customs. 5. Folklore—New York (State) 6. Parapsychology—New York (State)
  I. Title.
    QL89.H354 2013
    001.944—dc23
                          2013019601

To Rosa, my skeptical sweetheart,
Susan, my sister in the quest, and
the memory of Martha Hallenbeck,
the wisest and most wonderful grandmother ever

CONTENTS

INTRODUCTION: WILDER THAN YOU MIGHT THINK

"I offer the data. Suit yourself."—Charles Fort

onsters? In New York? Highly improbable, you may say. Surely New York is far too heavily populated to contain such cryptozoological beasties as lake monsters, bigfoots, and catamounts. Such things may exist in the wilds of Scotland or the Pacific Northwest, but not in the crowded northeast . . . right?

Wrong. New York City may have a population of more than 8.1 million, but that teeming metropolis only encompasses the southeastern tip of the state. The most crowded city in the United States comprises more than 40 percent of New York State's population. The farther upstate one travels, the wilder and more remote the countryside gets. Just outside of Manhattan lie the foothills of the Catskill Mountains, a region of myth and legend since pre-colonial times. The Hudson Valley is the setting for Washington Irving's famous stories of Rip Van Winkle and the Headless Horseman, among many other old folktales that still capture the imaginations of tourists and residents alike.

Farther north lie the Adirondack Mountains, now a forest preserve protected by the state. Adirondack Park covers 6.1 million acres, an area larger than the state of Vermont. It is, in fact, the largest park and the largest state-level protected area in the country, as well as the biggest National Historic Landmark. Champ, also known as the Lake Champlain Monster, is said to reside here. There have also been numerous sightings of bigfoot-type creatures in the Adirondack region. Mountain lions, long thought to be extinct in New York, may still lope throughout the state's many dense forests. My hometown of Kinderhook may even be inhabited by something the locals call "The Kinderhook Creature," a man-beast that terrorized a number of people in that old Dutch village back in the 1980s.

Along with the earthbound monsters, New York has also seen its share of alien creatures and "little people" from the days of Rip Van Winkle to today. Some believe these little people are related to alien abductions in the Hudson Valley and beyond.

We now travel to a land that many out-of-staters are completely unfamiliar with, a land that Native Americans claimed was inhabited by stone giants and horned serpents, and one that may be home to living plesiosaurs and undiscovered primates. From alligators in the sewers to the Montauk Monster, New York is stranger—and wilder—than you might think.

Ice Cannibals, Stone Giants, and Horned Serpents: Native American Folklore

ong before the Europeans colonized North America, the Mohawk and Abenaki tribes held sway in the area that would become New York State. The Mohawks were the most easterly tribe of the Iroquois confederation, while the Abenaki were one of the Algonquian-speaking tribes of the northeast. Their myths and legends were told and retold, and many of them are still known today.

Take the legend of the wendigo (or windigo), for example. A creature that appeared in the legends of the Algonquians, the wendigo was an evil, cannibalistic spirit in some stories, while in others it was a monster that human beings could become. In either case, it was associated with winter and the cold. One description of the fearsome creature comes from Basil Johnson, an Ojibwe scholar from nearby Ontario:

> The wendigo was gaunt to the point of emaciation, its desiccated skin pulled tautly over its bones . . . its complexion the ash gray of death, and its eyes pushed back deep into their sockets . . . like a skeleton recently disinterred from the grave. What lips it had were tattered and bloody . . . [it] gave off a strange and eerie odor of decay and decomposition, of death and corruption.

Although stories of the wendigo may have originated from times of famine, when tribes were forced into cannibalism, the creature has also been associated with what we would now call bigfoot or Sasquatch. The wendigo was introduced into horror fiction in Algernon Blackwood's classic 1910 story, "The Wendigo," and Stephen King referenced it in his novel *Pet Sematary*. It is a fearsome supernatural being by all accounts, and there is even a psychological condition called "Wendigo Psychosis," in which those who suffer from it develop an overwhelming desire to eat human flesh.

Frightening as it was, the wendigo was far from the only mythical creature that was spoken of around the fire by the Native American medicine men. The Wabanaki spoke of a similar being called, alternatively, the chenoo, the giwakwa, or the kiwakwa. By whatever name, it was thought to have been a human being who, through black magic, had been transformed into a flesh-eating giant. More akin to what we would call a bigfoot than the wendigo, these cannibalistic ogres would tower over the trees; they had enormous fangs and sometimes, in their ravenous hunger, ate their own lips. Their scream was so terrifying that any human who heard it would die of fright. Like the wendigo, they usually appeared in winter.

Strangely enough, the "ice cannibals," as they were sometimes called, got their evil powers from a lump of human-shaped ice in their stomachs. The only way to destroy the creatures was to chop them up into tiny bits so they would not regenerate.

Another "mythical" creature, the horned serpent, appears in the legends of many North American tribes. The Abenaki referred to it as Pita-Skog, or "Great Snake." Interestingly enough, stories of this creature correspond very closely with old Norse traditions of something called a Lindworm, meaning "dragon" or "sea serpent."

The Iroquois and the Abenaki both told stories about such a creature living in Lake Champlain, a huge glacier-created lake situated on the New York-Vermont border with its northernmost tip in the Canadian province of Quebec. The Abenaki called the creature "Tatoskok." The creature was said to lurk in Lake Champlain and to devour humans. Also known as "Gitaskog," the name literally means "great serpent" or "horned serpent." Although one theory has it that this tradition arose from a spot called Split Rock in Essex, New York—a natural rock structure that resembles petrified snakes—the stories are so widespread that one's natural inclination may be to believe that there really was, and perhaps still is, some type of "horned serpent" lurking in the depths of Lake Champlain.

Ancient petroglyphs in neighboring Vermont depict a creature that looks very much like what is now referred to as "the Lake Champlain Monster," or, more affectionately, "Champ." Tatoskok was described as having horn-like protuberances on its massive head, in much the same way that Champ is depicted today.

The Abenaki and other tribes told stories of all manner of fantastic creatures, including the culloo, a legendary bird of prey that was so enormous it could carry off a child in its talons. Could stories like these be race memories of flying reptiles such as pterodactyls? Legends of the so-called "thunderbird" pervade Native American tribal folklore.

In Wabanaki legends, Glooscap was a mythical cultural hero, somewhat akin to King Arthur in the mythology of the British Isles. He was a warrior against evil, and one of his many adventures involved battling a gigantic frog-monster that had swallowed all of Earth's water. Glooscap saved the world when he tackled the frog-monster. "The mountains shook," so the story goes, when the two titans clashed. Once Glooscap had disposed of the evil frog-monster, all of the waters were released back into the sea, and some animals were so relieved to see the waters back that they jumped into the ocean and became aquatic. This was the Native American explanation of how fish came to be.

These oral traditions were always colorful and full of magic and adventure, and the variety of monsters and creatures described in them is staggering. There was something called a water panther, a cross between a cougar and a dragon, that lived in deep water and caused people to drown. The eastern tribes also feared a ghost called "Flying Head," an undead monster that is created when an angry man kills his unfaithful wife. A Flying Head then rises from the woman's grave, avenging herself upon her husband and terrorizing others.

Obviously, the story of Flying Head is just that—a story. But other legends may have a basis in fact. For example, some believe that Native American stories of the "Stiff-Legged Bear," also known as "Big Man-Eater," could be a memory of mastodons, passed down through the generations long after those Ice Age animals became extinct. Some southeastern tribes used their native word for Big Man-Eater when they were shown pictures of African elephants by early explorers. Elephants do have a stiff-legged gait, with their legs positioned vertically under their bodies, unlike other animals such as bears. They also have very large heads, and Stiff-Legged Bear is usually described as having a head that is disproportionately large. Elephants can push over trees, as Stiff-Legged Bear is purported to have done.

After all the stories of wendigos and cannibalistic ice giants have been put to rest, there still remain beliefs among many Native American tribes that there is a wild, hairy, manlike creature living in the forest. The term "Sasquatch" is a word derived from the Salish, a West Coast tribe. But the East Coast has its stories too. In the bigfoot legends of some tribes, the Sasquatch are a race of shy, benign creatures. They may steal things from humans—including, sometimes, their wives—but they generally don't harm people and sometimes even help them.

Some tribes consider Sasquatch guardians of nature. As has been noted in modern bigfoot accounts, the creatures usually appear alone or in small family groups. They may exchange gifts with humans or use sign language to communicate with us. Yet other tribes describe these quasi-mystical beings as dangerous beasts that attack humans and may even, occasionally, devour them. These deadlier versions of bigfoot were known as Stick Indians or Bush Indians. They were sometimes found in large social groups or even their own villages, and they sometimes waged war on neighboring Native American tribes.

As we shall see in subsequent chapters, there is far more evidence for the existence of both bigfoot and lake monsters than what is contained in old tribal folktales. The Native Americans thought of these creatures as just another part of nature. They may have been absolutely correct in this belief.

Champ and Other Lake Monsters

 andra Mansi showed Champ to the world. Mansi, a soft-spoken tinsmith and amateur photographer from Vermont, became an overnight celebrity in 1981 when a photo she took of something large and animate in Lake Champlain was published in the *New York Times* and *Time* magazine. The photo appeared to show part of a dinosaur-like body, capped by a long neck and small head, rising up out of the waters of the lake.

The picture was taken on July 5, 1977, as Mansi and her future husband and their two children were picnicking and sightseeing along the waters of Lake Champlain on the Vermont side, just north of the town of St. Albans. It was a beautiful summer day, and so they all decided to cut across a field to get a better look at the lake. The children wasted no time in getting into the water and playing. While Mansi watched them, something else caught her eye.

Mansi saw a large object in the water out toward the middle of the lake. At first, she thought it might have been an immense fish, but she soon realized that she was actually seeing the long neck and grayish-brown head of some sort of creature. She noticed that the head seemed to be looking around, scanning the surrounding countryside. She recalled later that she was "scared to death," but she still had the presence of mind to grab her Kodak Instamatic camera from her car and snap one shot of the creature. A moment after she took the picture, they all got into the car and sped away from the lake.

Mansi later told cryptozoologist Loren Coleman that the beast she saw had "skin like an eel" and was "slimy-looking." She was afraid to tell anyone about the sighting for fear of ridicule and she hid the photo for three years. It wasn't until the growing investigation into the phenomenon of "Champ," the Lake Champlain Monster, that she began to talk with pioneering cryptozoologist Joseph W. Zarzynski, a high school teacher from Wilton, New York, about her encounter. Zarzynski had taken it upon himself to investigate the possible denizen of Lake Champlain with side-scan sonar and by diving into the lake's murky waters.

What Mansi saw that day in 1977 was a creature that had been sighted for centuries in Lake Champlain. Like the Loch Ness Monster, aka "Nessie," its cousin across the pond, Champ had been a legend among the locals. Native American tribes such as the Iroquois and the Abenaki were familiar with the beast. Once the Europeans arrived, the lake was named after French explorer Samuel de Champlain. He is often credited with having been the first European to see the monster, supposedly recording his experience in his journal entry for July 1609, in which he allegedly wrote of having observed a "serpentine" creature approximately twenty feet long, "as thick as a barrel" and with a "horse-like" head. Sadly, this story seems to be bogus, as it has only been traced as far back as the summer 1970 issue of *Vermont Life* magazine and an article written by Marjorie L. Porter. Champlain's actual journal entry referred only to "a great abundance of many species of fish . . . I have seen some five feet long, which were as big as my thigh."

The early settlers found that Lake Champlain held many mysteries. Comprising parts of New York, Vermont, and Quebec, Lake Champlain is nearly 110 miles long and thirteen miles wide, with a depth of four hundred feet at its deepest point. It is the largest freshwater lake in the United States, aside from the Great Lakes. Carved by glaciers during the last Ice Age, it shares many resemblances to Loch Ness, Okanagan Lake in British Columbia (home of another lake monster, "Ogopogo"), and dozens of glacier-created lakes around the world that are reputed to be home to various "monsters."

If we discount the Samuel de Champlain "report," the first sighting of Champ by Europeans still goes back quite a long way, to July 24, 1819, when the *Plattsburgh Republican* reported that settlers around the lake were alarmed by a huge creature that stuck its head above water at Bulwagga Bay, near what is now the town of Port Henry, New York. The article noted that a "Capt. Crum" sighted "an enormous serpentine monster."

Crum described the beast as "a black monster" roughly 187 feet long, with a flat head that resembled that of a seahorse. According to his account, the creature reared its head more than fifteen feet above the water; he noted that it was some two hundred yards away from him and that it traveled "with the utmost velocity" as it was pursued by "two large Sturgeon and a Bill-fish." Crum got a good enough look at the "monster" to see that it had three teeth, eyes "the color of a peeled onion," a white star on its forehead, and a red band around its neck.

In the 1870s, passengers on ferry steamships began to see the mysterious creature as they crossed the lake. Up to that point, few people had made their homes near the lake, but as the area became more settled, more and more residents claimed they saw a "monster" rising up out of its depths.

Author Robert E. Bartholomew uncovered several early sightings for his 2012 book, *The Untold Story of Champ: The Social History of America's Loch Ness Monster*. One was a spectacular sighting off Dresden, just north of Whitehall, reported in the July 9, 1873, edition of the *Whitehall Times*. A work gang laying down a railroad track sighted a huge serpentine creature just offshore. The article included a vivid description of the beast:

> As he rapidly swam away, portions of his body, which seemed to be covered with bright silver-like scales, glistened in the sun like burnished metal. From his nostrils he would occasionally squirt streams of water above his head in an altitude of about twenty feet. The appearance of his head was round and flat, with a hood spreading out from the lower part of it like a rubber cap often worn by mariners with a cape to keep the rain from running down the neck. His eyes were small and piercing, his mouth broad and provided with two rows of teeth, which he displayed to his beholders. As he moved off at a rate of ten miles an hour, portions of his body appeared above the surface of the water, while his tail, which resembled that of a fish, was thrown out of the water quite often.

The witnesses went on to state that the creature was "twenty or more feet long, and at least twenty inches in diameter." According to the report, the "monster" skimmed along the surface of the lake for roughly a quarter mile before vanishing into its depths.

Also in 1873, J. A. Parker of Whitehall told the *Whitehall Times* that he had had an encounter with the "sea serpent" some eight years earlier. Parker related to the newspaper that he had been traveling on the road two miles east of the village when he saw "a large snake eighteen to twenty feet long, and as large as a man's thigh emerge from the mountain recesses and move swiftly across the fields at the rate of ten miles an hour toward Jerry Collins' marsh, and take to the water." As Parker was a respected citizen, his report was taken very seriously.

When master showman P. T. Barnum of Barnum and Bailey's Circus got wind of these "Lake Champlain Sea Serpent" reports, he sent a letter to the *Whitehall Times*, in which he made the following offer: "I hereby offer $50,000 for the hide of the great Champlain serpent to add to my Mammoth World's Fair Show. You are authorized to draw on me for any sum necessary in securing the Monster's remains."

Needless to say, this raised excitement about the "monster" to a fever pitch, and there were now armed groups of men looking for the elusive beast near the shore. With a reward being offered for its hide, the creature seemed to take on a new "respectability."

There was an extraordinary encounter involving a steamboat on July 25, 1873. The *W. B. Eddy* was traveling from Ticonderoga to Whitehall when witnesses claimed it was struck by the "sea serpent" and nearly overturned. First Mate Kin Holcomb reported that he and the frightened passengers could clearly see the beast's head and neck some thirty yards away before it swam off as rapidly as "a fast sailing steamboat." The first mate thought they had struck a log until the ship shifted suddenly to one side. According to the newspaper report: "The passengers all made a rush to the opposite side of the boat when the vessel suddenly righted and the spectators were horrified at observing the head of a great snake rise from the water about 100 feet to their stern and spurt two jets of water high into the air." Holcomb also noted that the creature's "bright scales sparkled in the sun."

On September 28, 1881, the *Plattsburgh Sentinel* reported that three students from Burlington, Vermont, were sailing to the New York side of the lake when they encountered the monster near Juniper Island "making directly from the island to Port Kent. It was upward of seventy-five feet long." The head was reported as rising from six to eight feet out of the water.

In July 1883, Sheriff Nathan H. Mooney was observing the lake and happened to look off to the northwest area of the New York side when he saw a "gigantic water serpent" about fifty yards away. The creature rose about five feet out of the water and was from twenty-five to thirty feet in length, according to Mooney, who said that it was close enough for him to "clearly see that there were round white spots inside its mouth."

Bartholomew recounted a story from the *Plattsburgh Sentinel* of mid-August 1886, in which "a party of three" stood on the wharf of the Plattsburgh Dock Company one sunny afternoon when "twenty rods off they saw a creature fifteen feet long with its head and neck two feet above the water as it swam." The head was estimated to be approximately fifteen to eighteen inches in length.

Bartholomew also uncovered a story from historian Connie Pope of an incident that occurred three days after the "party of three" had their encounter. Three other men were fishing off a Plattsburgh dock when they reported that a "sea serpent" became hooked on one of the fishermen's lines. According to Pope: "Being unequal to the task of hauling it in he cried for help, and his two companions set their brawny backs to pulling with him. Together they raised to the surface the head of a horrible creature, at which point the line broke and the creature disappeared."

In October 1886, the *Plattsburgh Republican* featured a story on two recent sightings. The first involved a duck hunter from St. Albans who encountered something in the water much larger than his quarry: "He saw but a short distance away an enormous serpent coiled up on the swampy shore," and it looked to the man as though the creature were sleeping.

Then, "He reached back to get his gun and in doing so made a slight noise . . . the serpent reared his head fiercely and ran off toward a tangle of undergrowth, making as much noise, as he went crashing through the bushes, as a large hound would."

The second incident was reported by a couple who were riding by horse and buggy through Cumberland Head. They stopped, tied up their horse, and strolled around the beach where they saw "a creature with a snakelike head" in the lake. They estimated that the head protruded some eighteen inches above the water. The man picked up some stones and threw them at the creature, which hurriedly swam away.

In mid-October of that year, the *Plattsburgh Sentinel* featured an article on the front page that announced a $1,000 reward "to any person who will bring to this office, dead or alive, the Lake Champlain Sea Serpent." There was one caveat: the "monster" had to measure at least twenty feet in length. Needless to say, the prize, like that offered by Barnum, was never collected.

On August 4, 1892, a "monster" surfaced near the annual gathering of the American Canoe Association at Willsborough, New York, which brought a speedy conclusion to the celebration as the canoeists "scattered in panic." A September 27, 1894 story in the *Essex County Republican* recounted a land sighting of "the Lake Champlain Sea Serpent." Luther Hagar, Tim Miller, Frank Dominy, and Ephraim Allen encountered the beast at Cumberland Head near Plattsburgh. According to the article, "It caused a great commotion in the water . . . and came toward the shore and out of the water six feet or more upon the land."

In 1915, the *New York Times* reported that several observers saw the "sea serpent" stranded in the shallows of Bulwagga Bay, near Crown Point, New York. The creature was said to have been forty feet long and it "lashed the waters" in an attempt to escape back to the depths. It ultimately released itself from the shallow water and swam toward the Vermont side of the lake, until it sank "submarine fashion, leaving a wake which was well defined on the glassy surface of the lake."

On July 16, 1929, an article appeared in the *Charleston [West Virginia] Daily Mail* entitled "Sea Serpent Seen, Fishermen Assert." The feature went on to describe the experience of three young fisherman who "insisted they had seen the famous Lake Champlain sea serpent" near Willsboro, New York. Thomas Bridge and his two companions, Davis Riley and Wesley Quimby, were fishing at the mouth of the Boquet River on July 14, when what appeared to them to be "a huge serpent or fish thrust its head high above the surface of the lake." According to the witnesses, the "monster" began to violently shake its tail, "lashing the water for acres around in a sea of foam." The newspaper noted: "Terrified by the spectacle, Bridge did not stop running until he had reached the village, two miles away. Riley and Quimby also retired precipitously."

After that little appearance for the locals, Champ seems to have remained submerged for ten years, finally resurfacing in August 1939, when a Mr. and Mrs. Langlois were fishing from their motorboat near Rouses Point, New York. This turned out to be an uncomfortably close observation, as the "monster" swam in their direction; they quickly took off in their boat to avoid a collision with the beast. As they escaped to the shore, the creature slowly submerged under the lake's surface.

Champ returned to Rouses Point in 1943, when Charles Weston viewed it through binoculars from the shore. In the spring of 1961, a sighting of the creature was reported by Thomas E. Morse in North West Bay near Westport, New York. Writing of his experience many years later, Morse recounted, "When first seen it appeared as a massive gunmetal gray approximately eighteen inches wide . . . It appeared to be a monstrous eel with white teeth that raked rearward in the mouth." Morse saw the beast from his car as he was driving along the shore. He reported that the creature came up onto the shore and lifted its head around four feet, perhaps startled by the noise of Morse's car.

Then the beast lay low for a decade until 1971, when Joseph Zarzynski—known as "Zarr" to his friends—formed The Lake Champlain Phenomena Investigation. Zarzynski, a six-foot-four gentle giant with an easygoing manner, proved instrumental in getting witnesses to open up about their experiences. They didn't need to fear being ridiculed anymore; they now had a sympathetic ear.

As a result, many more eyewitnesses have come out of the woodwork in the past few decades. Zarzynski heard from a credible witness who had observed two dark humps swimming in the lake near Fort Ticonderoga in 1980. Another sighted a creature approximately twenty-five feet long near Port Henry in April 1981.

Ultimately, the Mansi photograph has been one of the most important pieces of evidence in arguing for the existence of Champ. After its national media appearances, Champ became something of a cryptozoological star that attracted interest from such luminaries as Dr. Roy Mackal, a University of Chicago zoologist who had done fieldwork at Loch Ness, and the University of Arizona's J. Richard Greenwell, the founder of the International Society of Cryptozoology (ISC). Greenwell was instrumental in obtaining a computer analysis of Mansi's photo, which concluded that the picture was of a genuine object and was not a case of so-called "trick photography."

When the *New York Times* published Mansi's photo on June 30, 1981, in an article entitled "Is It Lake Champlain's Monster?" it seemed as though there was no question that "something" lurked in the lake. As John Noble Wilford's feature revealed: "The analysis [of the photo] has now been completed, and the Arizona optical scientists confirm that the picture has not been tampered with . . . According to Dr. B. Roy Frieden, professor of optical sciences at Arizona, Mrs.

Mansi's photograph was a high-quality print that 'does not appear to be a montage or superposition of any kind' and the 'the object belongs in the picture.'"

Zarzynski was also quoted in the article; in fact, he received the last word: "I've never seen it myself . . . I know there are theories that explain it away, the most common being that it's a large sturgeon. But some of these sightings are tough to shoot holes in. The Mansi picture is the first clear-cut photograph of Champ that I'm aware of. It really puts the cap on things."

As of 2012, there have been more than three hundred reported sightings of Champ. After the Mansi photo, the most intriguing bit of evidence may be some audio recordings gathered by animal communication scientist Elizabeth von Muggenthaler, a former skeptic who became interested in the Champ legend after growing up around Lake Champlain and hearing stories of sightings told to her by friends and relatives. Beginning in 2003, she applied her particular science of bioacoustics to Lake Champlain, attempting to uncover any unusual sounds that may emanate from the depths of the lake.

In an article entitled "Searching for Champ," posted on Loren Coleman's Cryptomundo website in 2012, von Muggenthaler was quoted as saying: "Quite possibly the only way to discover a creature like this, if indeed one exists, is by recording it . . . Creatures that need to find underwater any sort of food or to navigate in a deep, dark, murky, cold lake would have to use advanced biosonar or echolocation."

Von Muggenthaler was referring to the aural communication used by whales and dolphins to navigate. Her theory was brought to the attention of the National Geographic Channel, which sent a production team to the lake for a TV series called *Wild Case Files*. Von Muggenthaler and her assistants did indeed record some strange sounds in Lake Champlain's depths. She continued: "When we detected echolocation in Lake Champlain . . . we recognized that there was something unique . . . Take into consideration as well that at least twenty beluga whale skeletons from 14,000 years ago have been unearthed intact from the Lake Champlain basin from when it was a sea. Could there be a population of creatures in there? Absolutely."

Von Muggenthaler pointed out that, judging by the frequency and amplitude of the acoustical signals she recorded, Champ may indeed be related to beluga whales. "Just like my voice is a different pitch than yours is, we know that we have recorded several different animals . . . It is clearly echolocation. We know by cross-correlation analysis that the creature sounds a lot like a beluga whale but is not exact, nor is it exactly killer whale nor exactly dolphin."

Von Muggenthaler claimed she has seen the creatures underwater, describing them as "humpy" and exhibiting "herding behavior." Sadly, she did not capture her sightings on video, but the quest continues.

In 2007, Champ once again made national headlines when ABC News broadcast a report that included a new video taken of the creature. During the summer of 2006, two respected local fishermen, Peter Bodette and Dick Affolter, took a video of a "strange wake" in Lake Champlain. Before their sighting, both men had been skeptical of the creature's existence, but Bodette told ABC News: "It was as big around as my thigh . . . I'm 100 percent sure of what we saw. I'm not 100 percent sure of what it was."

Affolter noted, "What we saw always stayed at the surface and parts of it would come above the water, like the back of the nose or the head." ABC News reporter Jim Avila seemed genuinely impressed with the footage and opined, "There is something in the water . . . just under the surface."

One of the better shots in the video shows something that has a dorsal fin just underneath the surface of the water. As with the Mansi photo, it appeared there had been no tampering with the video. Two retired FBI analysts reviewed the tape for ABC, and forensic image analyst Gerald Richards admitted, "I can't find anything in there that would suggest or indicate to me that this has been fabricated or manipulated in any way. However, there's no place in there that I can actually see an animal or any other object on the surface."

In 2009, multiple witnesses sighted Champ off Platts-burgh's Wilcox Dock. Carl Roberts and some friends were fishing off the dock on June 4 when a movement out on the lake caught their attention. Something large was moving in the water around one hundred yards beyond the dock. According to an article in the *Press Republican* of June 6, Roberts noted, "It had to be fifty feet long, from what I could see of the humps (rising above the lake's surface) . . . There was no wind, no boats, no explanation whatsoever. It was so close that I could see the texture of its skin."

Roberts's girlfriend attempted to snap a picture with her cell phone, but it was low on batteries and she couldn't get a shot. The group observed the creature as it moved toward the peninsula south of the dock. Roberts continued, "It didn't move like a snake . . . It was not like a porpoise or dolphin, either. It moved straight and fast, with its humps up high and then down lower in the water. I've never seen anything like it before."

It's interesting to note that Roberts, owner of a furniture shop in Plattsburgh, grew up at Cumberland Head and had seen twenty-foot-long lake sturgeon on some of his previous fishing excursions. Skeptics often point to sturgeon, misidentified by witnesses, as possible candidates for Champ. Roberts was adamant that what he saw on this occasion was no sturgeon.

Roberts said that the creature's skin was "whale-like" and had a shiny greenish-black tint. "It was no log, no boat, no animal I've seen before. I just can't believe it. I couldn't sleep because of it," Roberts claimed.

Obviously, all of these sightings beg the question: what is Champ? Skeptics have a cast of suspects, mainly sturgeon (which look nothing like the creatures described), otters (which sometimes play follow-the-leader with each other and may give the illusion of being one long snakelike creature), and even floating logs. Skeptics also point to the fact that, as Champ could not be just one immortal specimen, there must be a breeding colony of such creatures in the lake. Yet no carcasses have ever been found. Zarzynski, who ultimately wrote the definitive book on the subject, admitted, "The definitive thing to have is a carcass."

The non-skeptics also have several theories. J. Richard Greenwell, who passed away in 2005, was a proponent of the most popular—and as Zarzynski has noted, the "most romantic"—theory: that Champ is a surviving plesiosaur. Greenwell justified this theory by hypothesizing that some species of plesiosaur, not just in Lake Champlain but in Loch Ness and other Northern Hemisphere lakes, was trapped in inland lakes formed at the end of the last ice age. Allegedly, all plesiosaurs died out around 65.5 million years ago. But if Greenwell's theory is correct, and they survived beyond the last ice age, then perhaps they were warm-blooded animals— as indeed, more and more, the belief among scientists is that dinosaurs were warm-blooded, not cold-blooded as previously thought.

British cryptozoologist Karl P. N. Shuker theorizes that surviving plesiosaurs may have evolved to survive the colder temperatures in northern lakes, and that their neck structure might have evolved as well, which, according to Champ eyewitnesses, would allow them to raise their heads and necks out of the water like swans. Admittedly, this is a lot of theorizing without any proof; yet one look at the Mansi photo suggests something that looks very much like a plesiosaur.

Fellow cryptozoologist Roy P. Mackal, however, postulates a theory that many of the worldwide lake monster sightings, including those in Lake Champlain, may be explained as sightings of surviving zeuglodons. The zeuglodon, or basilosaurus

("King Lizard"), was actually a type of prehistoric whale that averaged around sixty feet in length and is believed to have been the largest animal to have lived in its time, which was forty to thirty-four million years ago. Its long, snakelike appearance could account for the "Lake Champlain sea serpent" appellation, and whales were mammals, so living in cold temperatures would be no problem for them. One tantalizing piece of evidence that could point to Champ being a zeuglodon is the fact that some fossils of the species were discovered near Charlotte, Vermont, a town near the lake. Mackal feels that these primitive whales may have access to the sea via waterways, which would explain why they only seem to appear at certain times of the year in the lake, and could also help explain why a breeding population may not have to live in the lake itself.

One spectacular example of a creature that has survived from prehistoric to modern times is that of the coelacanth, a type of Devonian fish that was thought to have gone extinct some 400 million years ago, but which was found alive off the coast of South Africa in 1938. Considered a "living fossil," the coelacanth has hardly evolved at all in those hundreds of millions of years.

Other candidates for Champ, according to cryptozoologists, are giant eels, which could account for some sightings but don't seem to precisely fit the descriptions of the beast. Pinnipeds, more commonly referred to as seals, are yet another possibility, suggested by several notable researchers, including Bernard Heuvelmans, the late Belgian–French scientist who is often called "the father of cryptozoology." Heuvelmans, as well as British paleontologist Darren Naish, theorized that an unknown species of large, long-necked pinnipeds may have evolved and could be responsible for alleged "sea monster" sightings, as well as sightings in lakes such as Champlain. Both Champ and Nessie have appeared on land on rare occasions, which makes this an appealing theory, but again, there is no real proof.

Researcher Dennis Hall, who claims to have seen Champ twenty times, postulates that Champ may be a tanystropheus, a long-necked prehistoric reptile from the Middle Triassic period, some 232 million years ago. Hall claims that, in 1976, his father caught a strange-looking reptile on the shores of Lake Champlain. He took the carcass to scientists, who concluded that it was like no living reptile they had ever seen. Unfortunately, this particular "fish" got away, and the specimen was somehow lost. When Hall later saw an illustration of a tanystropheus, he felt that it was very much like what his father had caught, and concluded that it would be an ideal candidate for Champ.

One point that skeptics always bring up is the lack of physical evidence. Why no Champ carcass? they ask. It's a fair question, and the most open-minded reply came from Dr. George Zug of the Smithsonian Institution in Washington, DC. Zarzynski quotes from Zug in his book *Champ: Beyond the Legend*, via Zug's paper that was delivered to a seminar on the existence of Champ on August 29, 1981: "If Champ were like dolphins, most deaths would occur in the winter and thus the probability of a stranding would be 'infinitesimal.'

"If a carcass did float ashore the likelihood of its discovery would be minimal. There are no regular patrols of the lake's shores as there are for reporting the stranding of all cetaceans on our ocean coast to allow the Smithsonian's marine mammalogist to accurately record cetacean stranding.

"Certainly the absence of a stranded carcass does not negate the possible existence of large aquatic animals; however, the absence does not support the existence of such creatures either."

Despite the lack of physical evidence, there have been enough reports of Champ sightings to encourage state and local governments to pass laws protecting the creature, even though it has not yet been proven to exist. The first such law was an ordinance passed in the Village of Port Henry, New York, on October 6, 1980. The resolution read, in part:

> Whereas, the existence of Champ has been documented by many of our North Country residents over the years and . . . Whereas, all endangered species are entitled to protection under both Federal and New York State laws . . . Now therefore, be it resolved by the Village Board of Port Henry that all the waters of Lake Champlain which adjoin the Village of Port Henry are hereby declared to be off limits to anyone who would in any way harm, harass or destroy the Lake Champlain Sea Monster.

The New York State Assembly passed its own "Champ Resolution" three years later, on April 18, 1983:

> Whereas. There are documented reports, historical accounts, and photographic evidence to substantiate the possible existence in Lake Champlain of an unidentified aquatic animal or animals described as long-necked, serpentine, or snakelike . . . Resolved. That the possible existence of the animal commonly known as "Champ" is recognized by this state . . . That "Champ" should be protected from any willful act resulting in death, injury or harassment . . . That the State of New York encourage serious scientific inquiry into the existence of any unusual animals in Lake Champlain . . . and be it further Resolved that citizens of New York and visitors to Lake Champlain are encouraged to report sightings of such animals or associated phenomena and photographic evidence whenever possible.

As a result of Port Henry's pioneering effort in protecting Champ, the village has erected a more or less full-sized statue of Champ and holds "Champ Day" on the first Saturday of every August. There is even a Facebook page for Champ Day, which reads in part: "The Village of Port Henry celebrates its most famous resident—Champ, the Lake Champlain creature—with an annual festival held the first Saturday in August.

"The downtown business district is the center of Champ Day activities. Merchants hold sidewalk sales and craftspeople sell their wares from booths along Main Street. It is the one place we can guarantee that you'll see Champ—you can even get him to pose for a picture."

The Facebook page is, of course, referring to posing for a picture with the Champ statue, not the real beastie. Your humble author may have come close to the creature once, although I didn't exactly get him to pose for a photograph. In the summer of 1983, I accompanied Zarzynski and his assistant, Pat Meaney, to Lake Champlain, where they had rented a cabin in Vergennes, Vermont. As I was mainly a "landlubber," my job was to run the side-scan sonar on shore while Zarzynski and Meaney dove into the depths in their scuba gear.

On one occasion, I was rather alarmed when, while I was running the sonar on the shore, I recorded something that looked to be approximately sixteen feet in length on the other side of an underwater ridge from where they were diving. When they came back up to the cabin, I showed them the sonar readings and they seemed quite surprised, and perhaps a little unsettled. While Zarzynski felt that what I recorded could have been a school of fish—although, to my untrained eyes, it looked like one solid object—he couldn't say for sure what it was . . . or what it was not.

I will, however, let Sandra Mansi have the last word on the question of Champ's existence. On August 29, 1981, Mansi attended a seminar entitled "Does Champ Exist?" in

Shelburne, Vermont. Forcefully, she announced to all the attendees of the conference: "You don't want to ask me if I think Champ exists. I've seen him, almost on a first-name basis. I've photographed Champ."

Although Champ is by far the most famous, it isn't the only water monster reported in New York State. As Loren Coleman pointed out in his book *Mysterious America*, the Oneida tribe told of how long ago a great serpent known as the "Mosqueto" dwelled in Onondaga Lake near Syracuse. This creature is now affectionately referred to as "Oggie." The lake, however, is now very polluted and the likelihood of a "monster" living there is remote. Onondaga Lake was once used for sewage disposal, and later for the disposal of the runoff from the nearby Nine Mile Island nuclear power plant, which would be enough to kill off most anything.

One of the few eyewitness sightings of Oggie occurred in 1977, when members of the Syracuse-area Cub Scout Troop 400 claimed to have seen something they described as a "dragon" swimming not far from the shore. Although most modern-day reports of Oggie amount to little more than urban legends, the creature is a local celebrity, appearing in the area's annual Halloween parades as a large fiberglass statue.

There was a famous hoax perpetrated at Lake George in the early twentieth century by painter Harry Watrous, who lived near the lake. Watrous had an ongoing rivalry with another resident, Col. William Mann, editor of a New York scandal sheet called *Town Topics*. According to the *Skeptical Inquirer*'s Joe Nickell, the two men competed over who could catch the largest trout, and on one fine day of fishing, Mann held up what appeared to be a forty-pound specimen as his boat passed by Watrous's boat. The artist later discovered that the fish was a fake made of painted wood. He decided to outdo Mann's hoax, as he recalled in 1934:

While the Colonel was in New York attending to business during the week ending June 27, 1904, I got a cedar log and fashioned one end of it into my idea of a sea monster or hipogriff. I made a big mouth, a couple of ears . . . four big teeth . . . and for eyes I inserted in the sockets of the monster two telegraph pole insulators of green glass.

I painted the head in yellow and black stripes, painted the inside of the mouth red and the teeth white, painted two red places for nostrils and painted the ears blue.

The log of which I fashioned the head was about ten feet long. To the bottom of the log I attached a light rope which I put through a pulley attached to a stone which served as an anchor. The pulley line was about 100 feet long and was manipulated from the shore.

Then Watrous anchored his "monster" close to the path that Mann's boat usually traveled and, after testing his creation several times, waited for his neighbor to arrive. Watrous later described the scene: "I watched as the launch approached and just as it was about ten feet away from my trap I released the monster. It came up nobly, the head shaking as if to rid itself of water, and I will say that to several people in Col. Mann's boat it was a very menacing spectacle."

News of the Lake George "sea serpent" spread quickly and Watrous deviously moved the "beast" from place to place along the lakeshore in front of as many witnesses as possible. Throughout the next few years, Watrous occasionally went out at night to make his "monster" known, always careful that no one ever got a clear look at it, especially reporters and photographers.

Perhaps tiring of the game, Watrous eventually packed up his "sea serpent" and it was more or less forgotten until 1920, when Louis Spelman of Silver Bay discovered the model at a local property sale. Taking it home with him, Spelman decided to return the "beast" to the water to see if the pulley mechanism still worked. It is said that the "monster's" appearance caused a near disaster on a ferry boat when nearly all the passengers rushed to one side to get a closer look. Spelman decided that playing with Watrous's creation was too dangerous, and he retired the "beast" permanently.

The Lake George Monster, affectionately known as—what else?—George, is now on display at the Hague Museum in the Hague Town Hall. It's actually a reproduction of Watrous's original, which seems to have vanished forever.

There is also a legend of "the Reptile of Cayuga Lake" in Ithaca. Since 1826, visitors to the lake have reported encounters with some sort of serpent that supposedly dwells in the lake's depths. In 1897, an article in the *Ithaca Journal* noted the sixty-ninth anniversary of one of the earliest Cayuga Lake monster sightings, relating that reporters from the newspaper were afraid to go to the lake's shores "due to the many reports of the frightening creature." The feature also noted that there had been many sightings of the creature since, which was described as an "undulating monster" between twelve and fifteen feet long.

A 1929 article in the same newspaper postulated a theory that the creature (or creatures) migrated into the lake through a "subterranean tunnel" that supposedly connected Cayuga Lake to Seneca Lake. Why Seneca Lake? Because a monster supposedly resides there too, and in fact it was alleged to have been captured in 1899.

Both Cayuga and Seneca Lakes are part of the Finger Lakes, a group of eleven lakes in the west-central section of New York State. Cayuga and Seneca are among the deepest bodies of water in North America. In an 1899 edition of the *New York Sun*, an account appeared that told of a stern-wheeled steamship that sailed the lake from nearby Geneva.

The captain of the paddleboat attempted to navigate his way around what at first appeared to be an overturned boat. When his passengers and crew gathered to take a look at the "boat," however, they realized that it was not another vessel at all, but rather a living creature that promptly swam away from the oncoming vessel.

The captain decided to take off in pursuit of this surprising beast, but the "monster" turned toward the boat, "reared its head upward, and revealed to those watching a forbidding set of sharp teeth." The feisty captain then ordered his crew to ram the beast, but they ended up playing a game of hide-and-seek with the creature, as it would come to the surface again and again, only to submerge when the boat got near it. Finally, however, the tenacious captain succeeded in ramming the creature and killing it.

The carcass was dragged back to shore and examined by a town doctor, who described it as being around twenty-five feet long, with a tapered tail, triangular head, and round eyes, and with a body encased in what looked like myriad turtle shells.

Ultimately, though, the story of the Seneca Lake Monster is a "fish story." No one knows what happened to the carcass. How does one lose a twenty-five-foot-long body? Supposedly, however, other individuals of this mysterious species have been seen in the lake over the years, so the true story of the Seneca Lake Monster is perhaps yet to be written.

And finally, there have been reports of a monster in New York's most famous body of water, the Hudson River. Known as "Kipsy," probably after the city of Poughkeepsie, sightings have been rare and there is no current scientific evidence supporting the existence of such a creature. A mural of Kipsy is on display at the National Art Honor Society in Poughkeepsie. According to their press release, "the ancient creature is believed to have existed and was said to have been sighted by sailors on many vessels including Henry Hudson's *Half Moon*, the Livingston's *Clermont* and even our own *Clearwater*."

Confirmed sightings of Kipsy are hard to come by, although the *New York Times* recorded sightings of "an unusually large manatee" in the river between Manhattan and Poughkeepsie in August 2006. Whether or not Kipsy really exists, New York State, as we have seen, has a grand tradition of river and lake monsters. Old traditions die hard, and the reason for their longevity may just be because there is something real behind them.

Perhaps the most bizarre "sea monster" encounter in New York, however, involved a known animal that was simply out of its natural habitat. In 1904, off the coast of the town of New Dorp in Staten Island, resident Frank Krissler and a friend were out fishing in their rowboat early in the morning when, according to the book *Weird New York* by Chris Gethard, the two men heard "an inhuman howl" that emanated from the water; the sound was so loud that it shook their boat. As Gethard wrote, "There was something huge in the water. And it was heading right toward them. At first, they thought it was an attacking whale."

The two men rowed like mad to reach the shore, but the leviathan kept up with them the entire way. They made it safely to the beach, but this was not the end of their fright. Whatever was following them was climbing up out of the water onto the shore!

And now the men realized what had made that ghastly bellow and what had been pursuing them: a fully grown elephant, which was "lumbering out of the briny deep and onto the beach with them." They could see, though, that the beast was not angry or ferocious, just befuddled—as they no doubt were themselves.

As one might expect, word spread fast—mainly from the elephant's bellows—and other fishermen arrived on the beach. They could see that the animal was in some distress, so they decided to help it by tying a rope around its tusks and leading it to the police station, "where the cops were just as surprised to see an elephant as the fishermen had been." The creature was placed in a stable, given food and water, and became an instant tourist attraction.

According to Gethard, by the end of the day the mystery had been solved: a gentleman who represented Luna Park in Brooklyn's Coney Island arrived, having heard about the elephant's sudden appearance, and explained that the gentle giant had escaped from the park, shambled into the sea, and somehow managed to swim six miles from Coney Island to New Dorp. Amazingly enough, two other elephants had also escaped and had made their way to Long Island!

The elephant was released to the park's representative and the animal was walked through town to a ferryboat that waited to take him to Brooklyn. The next day, the headline in the *New York Times* screamed: "Elephant Lands in Jail For Swimming Narrows."

Unexpected encounters with "monsters" don't get much stranger than that.

The Adirondack Bigfoot and Other Primates

It is probably easier for most people to believe that there may be unknown primates lurking in such far-flung places as the Himalayas and, perhaps, the American Northwest. Those areas contain miles and miles of remote forests and mountains where such beings as yeti and Sasquatch might roam. But what of the Adirondack Mountains of upstate New York?

Stories similar to the Algonquin legends of the "wendigo" or "windigo" were known throughout the North American continent, and the Adirondacks were no exception. To the Algonquin tribes, the wendigo was "a giant cannibalistic man" who made sounds "like that which grouse make when they drum." And once again, explorer Samuel de Champlain is credited with receiving some of the earliest reports of these creatures to fall on European ears.

This time, unlike in the case of Champ, it seems as though de Champlain actually did hear of these creatures. On his first exploration of North America, while traveling along the Saint Lawrence River in what is now upstate New York, he wrote in his journal of tales told to him by the Native Americans he encountered; they spoke of an immense, hairy, manlike creature they called the "Gougou." These creatures were spoken of so often that de Champlain believed there must indeed have been some sort of "devil" behind the stories. He was so convinced that the Gougou was real that he publicly spoke of it upon his return to France.

The original English translation of de Champlain's French journal logs reads, in part: "There is another strange thing worthy of narration, which many savages have assured me was true; this is, that near Chaleur Bay, towards the south, lies an island where makes his abode a dreadful monster, which the savages call Gougou . . . This monster . . . makes horrible noises in that island, and when they speak of him it is with utterly strange terror, and many have assured me that they have seen him . . . This is what I have learned about this Gougou . . . the tops of the masts of our vessels would not reach his waist."

Early settlers in New York and Vermont recorded encounters with a creature they called "Slippery Skin," which was said to resemble a huge bear, but with one important difference: it walked on two legs. Washington County historian and *Glens Falls Post-Star* newspaper columnist Paul Rayno noted in an article in the *Post Star* on March 26, 1975: "It ripped up fences and gardens, chased cows and sheep, dragged trees through cornfields and other crops, threw stones at school children and terrified hunters." Eyewitnesses noted that the creature had huge legs the size of "spruce logs," but that despite its imposing size, it was more mischievous than dangerous.

One of the earliest newspaper accounts of a northeastern bigfoot was published in the *Exeter Watchman* of September 6, 1818. The headline read, "Another Wonder," and the report went on to note that "an animal resembling the Wild Man of the Woods" had been seen near Ellisburgh in Jefferson County, New York, by "a gentleman of unquestionable veracity." The report went on to state that the creature "came from the woods within a few rods of this gentleman—that he stood and looked at him and then took his flight in a direction which gave a perfect view of him for some time. He is described as bending forward when running—hairy, and the heel of his foot narrow, spreading at the toes. Hundreds of persons have been in pursuit for several days, but nothing further is seen or heard of him."

The town of Moriah is inside Adirondack Park, and a bigfoot-like creature was reported near there in the later 1800s. In the 1920s, there was a report near Schroon Lake, which is also inside the park, by a couple named Wright. They claimed to have seen a "strange bear walking upright."

A decade later, in the Adirondack town of Blue Mountain Lake, there was a sensational series of Adirondack "wild man" sightings that drew national attention in February 1932. This "wild man," however, was all too human, although he may have been the first being to be labeled as "bigfoot" because his footprints were "nearly a yard across."

Post Star reporter Donald Metivier brought the story to light. The "wild man" had been blamed for burning down a number of lumber camps and cabins just north of Lake George. Two trappers, Dick Farrell and Reg Spring of Indian Lake, found an old lumber camp near Dunbrook Mountain and discovered that the so-called "wild man" was living in it. Forming a posse with some other men, they tried to get the "creature" to surrender to them, but it jumped out the window and ran off on the snow-covered ground, crouching behind a pile of logs and supposedly announcing, "I just want to be left alone. Go away." As the men got closer to him, they realized that indeed he was just a man—a man with a shotgun, in fact. The posse fired back and killed him. The "wild man" turned out to be a five-foot six-inch, 160-pound black man who had covered himself with several layers of untanned deer- and bearskins. To this day, his identity remains a mystery, although he was found to have been carrying Canadian currency. He was buried in Potters Field at North Creek in an unmarked grave.

Reports from the Adirondack region were few and far between for many years afterward. In 1959, Whitehall, New York farmer Harry Diekel's neighbor told him of seeing a bearlike creature on two legs. In the fall of 1967, near Ithaca, there was a major UFO wave. Mixed in with these sightings were reports of a big, hairy, bigfoot-type creature seen in the woods in the proximity of a UFO. There was even an unconfirmed report of one of these creatures tearing a young boy's jacket.

In nearby Watertown in 1975, there was an encounter by teenagers Steve Rich, Jerry Emerson, and another unnamed boy who claimed to have seen a five-foot creature "swinging its arms" when they were walking on State Street Hill. In May of that same year, Whitehall resident Clifford Sparks, owner of the Skeene Valley Country Club, encountered an eight-foot-tall, hairy, "sloth-like" creature near the first green of his golf course.

In the autumn of 1975, Whitehall police sergeant Wilfred Gosselin and his brother Russell heard an eerie, high-pitched scream that lasted for more than one minute while the pair was hunting at the intersection of Abair Road and Route 22A in Whitehall. Veteran hunters, they had never heard anything like it before. Around that same time, two men in Saranac Lake claimed to have seen a bigfoot squatting by Route 3. They started to approach it, but it walked away.

In 1976, the Adirondack Bigfoot really came into its own. The clamor began with a report in June from Watertown, where two boys reported that they had seen an eight-foot-tall creature covered in black hair. Fifteen-inch tracks were subsequently found in the area. In August, also near Watertown, two other teenage boys claimed to have seen a hairy, hulking creature in the woods.

It was in Whitehall, however, where the most spectacular sightings occurred that year. In fact, they remain the most extraordinary sightings of the Adirondack Bigfoot to this day.

A town of slightly more than four thousand people, Whitehall is located in Washington County amid the foothills of the Adirondack Mountains near Lake Champlain. In 1976, the population was even smaller—but, apparently, it included at least one bigfoot. On August 24 of that year, Whitehall residents Martin Paddock, Paul Gosselin, and Bart Kinney encountered something very strange in a field near Abair Road, just outside of town. Several years later, Gosselin told author and investigator Bill Brann about the incident, which Bartholomew recorded in his *Monsters of the Northwoods*.

Gosselin recalled: "It was about ten p.m. when Marty Paddock and I saw a large human form standing on the side of the road. We went to the end of the road, turned around and came back. We stopped and heard a sound like a pig squealing or a lady screaming. We drove off to the top of the hill, locked the doors on the truck, I loaded the gun and pointed it out the window. We turned around and drove to the opposite side of the road so I could have a better shot at it."

At first, the two men couldn't see anything in the darkness. Then, Gosselin saw the figure standing near a telephone pole about seventy feet away. Suddenly, he claimed, it began running toward their truck. "I couldn't speak," Gosselin told Brann. "Finally, I blurted out, 'Marty, get the hell out of here!'"

Paddock slammed the truck into gear and burned about fifty-seven feet of rubber down the road. They went to the Whitehall Police, but no one there would believe them—despite the fact that Gosselin's father, Wilfred, was a police sergeant, currently off-duty. The two men decided to meet with a friend, Bart Kinney, whom they told about their sighting and who agreed to accompany them to Abair Road. When they got there, the creature was still in the area.

Gosselin related: "It scared me—it scared me a lot. What really attracted me was the eyes on it; big red eyes. It just stood there. It didn't move . . . It was seven to eight feet tall, about 300 to 400 pounds, and it had thick, short, brown, coarse hair. On the head, longer hair. We returned and reported it to the Whitehall Police, who notified Whitehall State Police and the Sheriff's Patrol. There were eleven of us all together. Eight were police officers."

Although off-duty, Gosselin's father joined the group. Gosselin, father and son, walked into the field where the monster had been and then heard a frightening scream. A sheriff shone a spotlight onto the field and saw something walking along the fence. Paul Gosselin related, "He (the police officer) got a perfect look at it, but later he wouldn't admit it, afraid everyone would make fun of him."

Paddock also spoke to Brann about what has come to be known as the "Abair Incident." His description of the encounter ties in with Gosselin's: "[The creature] was standing on a knoll not far from the shoulder of the road. I really didn't get a good look at it then, but seeing it later, I would describe it as being seven to eight foot tall, weighing more than 300 pounds. It was muscular, big and stocky."

Kinney, the third member of the original group, also confirmed the sighting to Brann: "It was in the field 500 to 600 feet away. I never saw the face. It was about seven to eight feet tall and stooped from the shoulders as it walked. The creature was moving rather slow when I saw it. It was no bear, I know that. A bear doesn't walk like that."

Brian's older brother Paul was also a Whitehall policeman, and the following night he had his own encounter with the unknown creature. He later told Brann: "Myself and one of the state troopers were out there and I was turning around in the middle of the road and he was down the far end turning around. My headlights on the car picked up a pair of eyeballs. Big, red eyeballs, and I turned the lights of the car off. I shined my flashlight out there and that's when I (saw) the thing look right at me.

"I called the trooper on the C.B. He went up into the field where the creature had been seen and spotlighted the hedgerow. I turned off the lights and engine and waited in the dark. Something came crashing through the woods. I turned my headlights back on and the creature was about thirty feet in front of me. I stepped out of the car; the window was down on the driver's side."

Gosselin pulled his gun and was ready to fire, but didn't. He told Brann: "It was very human-like. You would have had to have been there to understand; then I could ask you the same question. All it did was stand there. It put its hands in front of its eyes. Hands? I don't know if that's what they were. I couldn't see any fingers. All it did was scream at the top of its lungs. I watched him for a good minute. Then he turned around and started back into the woods."

Paul Gosselin said the creature was, "About seven-and-a-half to eight feet tall and weighed about 400 pounds . . . It had big, red eyeballs that bulged about a half-inch off his face. As far as the mouth and nose, I didn't notice any. I was too scared and too shook up."

Scared as he may have been, Gosselin did notice a lot of other intriguing details: "It had no tail and it doesn't walk on all fours, it walks on two, like a man would. It's covered with hair, dark brown, almost black, and the back end of it, the hair was more or less worn off because you could see the cheeks of the buttocks through the hair that was more or less worn. He was covered with clay on the backside. His arms hung just eight to ten inches below his knees. He walks with a hunch . . . didn't run, although it could move fast."

The next morning, Paul and Brian Gosselin returned to the "scene of the crime" and found tracks in the matted grass that had a five-foot stride between them. They also found a large footprint in a streambed near the Poultney River.

That evening, an anonymous Whitehall High School official reported that he saw a large, hairy creature walking out of Bixby's Apple Orchard. The apelike beast crossed the road in front of his car and disappeared into the brush. On the same day, a sheriff's deputy and a state trooper found nineteen-inch tracks near the Poultney River Bridge. They made plaster casts of them; these casts still exist today.

Sightings continued in the Whitehall area. On August 30, another state trooper observed a large, hairy, apelike figure seventy-five to one hundred yards off in the field near Abair Road. An article published that day in the *Glens Falls Post-Star* headlined "Officers Track Creature" read, in part: "Police are investigating reports of a large, unidentified creature seen last week in the town of Whitehall . . . Although descriptions vary somewhat, the creature has been widely described by both police officials and civilians as between seven and eight feet tall, very hairy, having pink or red eyes, being afraid of light and as weighing between 300 and 400 pounds.

"It reportedly makes a sound that has been described as a loud pig's squeal or a woman's scream, or a combination."

In the midst of all this hysteria, a resident of the nearby town of Granville told Whitehall police, "I shot Bigfoot!" He and others claimed that they fired ten to twelve shots at the beast, but apparently their aim was off, as the creature was able to escape back into the depths of the woods.

On September 7, a state trooper found several nineteen-and-a-half-inch "human-like" tracks near the Poultney River in the Abair Road area. This was the last sign of bigfoot during that particular flap, but there were many more to come later.

One year later, in fact, Royal Bennett and his granddaughter Shannon noticed a "stump" in a field off Fish Hill Road in Whitehall. Suddenly, the "stump" stood up and they realized that it was a "honey-colored" creature, which they estimated to be seven to eight feet tall and weighing approximately five hundred pounds. It promptly walked off into the woods. Large humanoid tracks, thirteen and a half inches long, were discovered in the area by bigfoot researcher William Brann.

In July 1977, a family requesting anonymity found fourteen-inch footprints while camping near Big Eddy, near the Great Sacandaga Lake in the foothills of the Adirondacks. Meanwhile, back in Whitehall only a month later, a man walking his dog was terrified by "inhuman" screams outside his residence on Abair Road. The dog acted strangely, the man noted, as if it knew there was something very unusual about.

Two years later, on May 17, 1979, a man from Fair Haven, Vermont, along with his mother, father, and sister-in-law, observed a hairy, manlike head peering at them over bushes. The man yelled at the animal, whereupon the creature ran off with an "inhuman gait." About a week later, the man and the same group of relatives saw the creature again, this time while fishing on East Bay River.

Most people who reported these sightings preferred not to have their real names used. In 1979, again in Whitehall, a man identified only as Mr. "B" and his friend saw a big creature with a large stride walk "over" a fence. Around that same time period, a sheriff's deputy investigated reports of unearthly screams near a trailer park at Saratoga Lake. During the course of his investigation, he discovered a ten-inch diameter tree torn from the ground and thrown against one of the trailers.

Sightings in the region continued throughout the 1980s. In the winter of 1981, a cross-country skier found footprints with unusually long strides in the Adirondack Park region. Another area within the park, Bullhead Mountain near Indian Lake, had its own set of tracks in the snow that winter, discovered by a hunter who followed them for a mile. The hunter also found an odd cone-shaped hut in the area. A bigfoot residence, perhaps?

One of the few serious researchers involved in local bigfoot reports was Dr. Warren L. Cook, a professor of history and anthropology at Castleton State College just across the border in Vermont. Cook wrote the foreword to a book called *Monsters of the Northwoods*, co-written by Paul Bartholomew, his brother Robert, William Brann, and myself. Dr. Cook's foreword read in part: "The evidence for the species' existence and ongoing reproduction—if not guaranteed survival—in this area of North America is impressive in its historical depth and for the numerous incidents in the 1970s and 1980s . . . No one wants to be laughed at by their neighbors and it has been my experience that most sightings of hairy hominids in the northeastern U.S. go unreported in the media and have to be ferreted out by investigators."

Although nothing quite as spectacular as the Abair Road incidents has occurred again, reports of bigfoot-like creatures have persisted in the Whitehall and Lake George areas up to the present day. The creature has become so accepted among residents of Whitehall that, in 2003, Paul Bartholomew was instrumental in getting an ordinance passed to protect the species.

The "Sasquatch/Bigfoot Protective Ordinance" for Whitehall, New York, passed in both the Town and Village of Whitehall. It was largely symbolic legislation that worked on various levels. First, it was to honor the late Dr. Cook. In 1987, he had proposed through the office of then Vermont governor Madeleine Kunin that the Sasquatch be placed on the state's "endangered species" list. Although the measure was not passed, it was properly proposed to the Subcommittee on Mammals of the Vermont Endangered Species Committee. In a letter to Dr. Cook dated November 24, 1987, committee chairman Robert W. Fuller wrote that such a measure required "specific criteria" that was not met at that time:

"Implicit in the above, but lacking in this case, is a scientifically recognized taxon (species level) to which an organism can be referred. Understandably, I trust, the subcommittee is constrained in any consideration of cryptobiology in developing official lists of endangered or threatened species lest the credibility of the system and listings be destroyed.

"In closing, I should like to honor the integrity and hail the open-mindedness of our Subcommittee in considering a subject generally viewed with great skepticism.

"Without exception, members wished to express encouragement to you and to others whose research efforts may ultimately identify and document the existence of the 'Sasquatch.'"

Dr. Cook felt that these creatures should be protected at all costs because they could represent a glimpse into our own past. In an interview with Paul Bartholomew on May 9, 1989, Cook explained his thoughts on what he called this "cosmic species":

"My view is that we know so little about the population density of these creatures, that it is possible that the death of one single creature, of any age or either sex, might deprive that particular breeding pool of its ability to sustain itself. The breeding pools are obviously few in number and far apart, so the disappearance of any particular breeding pool, through a wanton act of shooting one, is a crime that's beyond condemnation—it's despicable."

Bartholomew told me his motivation behind advocating for the Whitehall legislation:

The [Whitehall] measure, which I wrote in 2003, was to honor the late Dr. Cook and his attempt to get Sasquatch put on the endangered or threatened species list as a protective measure. Also, it was written to draw the proper attention and perspective on the traditional histories of this alleged species. From the Algonquin, Iroquois, and Abanaki, to the journals of Samuel de Champlain, references to this creature are plentiful. The

"Gougou," "Windigo," "Stone Giants," "Old Slippery-skin," wild men, etc. So this phenomenon is clearly part of our heritage.

It also provided a platform for the community to embrace this enigma. For example, former Whitehall police officer Dan Gordon felt he had to remain quiet about his sighting of a creature in Whitehall due to the ridicule factor. It wasn't until more than twenty years later, and his retirement from the police force, that he publicly came forward with his account. It should be noted that his sighting was verified by a second anonymous law-enforcement official who was riding with Gordon at the time. Hopefully, the measure will encourage others to come forward with their account and the recognition of such respectable sightings will subside the ridicule effect this topic often garners.

The measure also presented an opportunity for Whitehall to promote eco-tourism to the region and generate a legitimate understanding of this sometimes complex and always controversial and mysterious community of elusive creatures. In that regard, with no revenues asked for, this is clearly a win-win for the community, tourists, and creatures alike.

Sightings of the Adirondack Bigfoot continue in and around Whitehall to this day. Bartholomew is always collecting new sightings and new information from eyewitnesses. On June 5, 2003, Larry Paap of nearby Granville contacted Bartholomew about his sighting in Comstock. While driving along Route 22A, Paap said that he saw a creature squatting in a field and that the creature was around four feet high in a crouched position, with "shoulder blades seeming pretty massive," and that its "arms were perched" on the ground. Paap said the creature disappeared after staring at him for about thirty seconds. "I couldn't figure out how it vanished," he told Bartholomew.

A couple on South Road in a rural area of Whitehall said that on the evening of June 18, 2003, they heard an "angry" vocalization outside their home and then caught a brief glimpse of a four- to five-foot-tall creature. The couple stated that the vocalizations were unlike anything they had heard before.

According to Bartholomew, one of the most impressive sightings was reported to him by two Chinese restaurant employees from bordering Clemons, New York. On a June morning in 2004, the two were fishing near a tavern when they spotted a "big, tall, and skinny" creature "standing" in about five feet of water. They could see the creature "from the waist up" and one of the gentlemen told Bartholomew, "I just told my friend before that I saw the monkey. I remember noise and sound (dogs barking) . . . then looked and (saw the creature) in the water up to its chest . . . then it moved very fast." The two men watched as the "brown and red" creature waded quickly through the water and disappeared out of sight. One of the witnesses said it looked like an orangutan with a "flat face." Bartholomew feels this sighting is significant because of the cultural background of the witnesses: "The witnesses said they simply were not aware that there were 'monkeys' in this area. That is particularly interesting since in their cultural expectation, it would have had a lesser effect on them, since they came from a region in which primates were expected. This is a particularly high-credibility report in which the gentlemen had nothing to gain and did not realize the significance of their encounter."

Another interesting encounter took place on August 18, 2006. A gentleman who preferred to remain anonymous told Bartholomew that he had seen a large creature standing near a fence behind a waste treatment plant near South Bay. The man reported, "I'm always looking for deer . . . I looked right over there behind the fence . . . and there's woods right there . . . (it was) reaching up like this, standing upright. . . . It was reaching for something . . . long arms, real sharp angles—like a forty-five degree angle. It was black, all black . . . shoulders were straight like a linebacker's . . . and a big bull neck . . . He had to be close to seven foot." The man ended his account by telling Bartholomew, "I didn't tell anyone else. You are the only one I've ever told other than my wife."

On Labor Day 2006, another incident occurred on Route 4 outside Whitehall. According to Bartholomew, "four very credible professional workers" saw a creature standing near the road. One witness reported, "It had a white face and black hair and stood about seven feet tall." The driver and his three passengers all saw the creature, gave corresponding descriptions, and drew "very similar" drawings of its likeness.

In August 2008, a fifteen-year-old girl saw a tall creature standing on the edge of the woods near Upper Turnpike Road. She described it as having "thick, long hair . . . [a] dark brownish color." She judged that it must have been "between seven and eight feet tall," and a few moments after the sighting, she and her mother both heard a "high-pitched screech."

In October of 2008, a man was driving his daughter to school shortly after 7 A.M. when they both observed a human-like creature cross the road in front of the car. It leapt from a rocky area and the girl said the creature turned its head toward them as it ran on two legs across the road and over an embankment.

As Bartholomew noted, "Sightings, vocalizations and track finds continue to be reported in and around the Whitehall region. They form a continual and consistent chain of reports from earlier times to the present."

The New York State Department of Environmental Conservation (DEC) disagrees with Bartholomew, however. In November 2012, Peter Wierner of the Chautauqua Lake Bigfoot Expo wrote to the DEC to seek protection for Sasquatch on a statewide basis. Gordon Batcheller of the DEC wrote back to Wierner, stating: "The mythical animal does not exist in nature or otherwise. I understand, however, that some well-organized hoaxes or pranks have occurred, leading some people to believe that such an animal does live. However, the simple truth of the matter is that there is no such animal anywhere in the world. I am sorry to disappoint you. However, no program or action in relation to mythical animals is warranted."

Some may say that is a government bureaucrat speaking platitudes from behind his desk. Far be it from me to make such a suggestion.

The Kinderhook Creature

Early on a December morning in 1978, my paternal grandmother, Martha Hallenbeck, looked through her kitchen window to see a "big, black, hairy thing all curled up" on her lawn. She told no one about her sighting at the time, afraid that they might think she was "seeing things." She just went about her business, and the next time she looked out the window, the thing was gone.

My grandparents lived, as did I, in the little town of Kinderhook, New York, about twenty miles south of Albany, the state capital. Located in Columbia County, Kinderhook is one of the oldest towns in the state; Henry Hudson and his crew of the *Half Moon* landed at the future town site as they traveled up the Hudson River in 1609. The name means "children's corner" in Dutch, as Hudson and his men were supposedly greeted on the shore by Native American children.

Kinderhook is noted as one of the more haunted places in the Hudson Valley, right up there with Sleepy Hollow. In fact, Washington Irving wrote most of his classic tale *The Legend of Sleepy Hollow* while living in Kinderhook. The town is steeped in history and folklore, and sometimes the two become intertwined. For example, Martin Van Buren, the eighth president of the United States, was born and is buried here. Supposedly, Van Buren popularized the expression "OK," which originally stood for "Old Kinderhook." And it should come as no surprise that his ghost reputedly haunts the grand old mansion of Lindenwald, his home in life, which is now a tourist attraction on Route 9H just south of town.

Despite growing up in this magical, mysterious environment, I was rather skeptical when I heard stories of a bigfoot-type creature roaming the area in the late seventies. I was most interested in the yeti of the Himalayas and the Sasquatch in the Pacific Northwest, but the idea of a creature like that in Kinderhook seemed ridiculous.

In 1978, however, there was an article in the *Hudson River Chronicle* concerning sightings of just such creatures in the nearby Columbia County towns of Canaan, Chatham, and Nassau. Late in 1978, mysterious footprints were discovered in the snow not far from my parents' home. My parents lived on the edge of a tangled forest and swampland known locally as Cushing's Hill. Nobody really knows why it's called that; in fact, some say the name is a bastardization of "Pincushion Hill," so called because of all the thorny trees and scrub to be found on the hill.

My cousin, Barry Knights, was only fourteen at the time, but was already an experienced hunter and trapper. He found a set of large three-toed tracks in the snow in December 1978. These were discovered on my grandparents' property, about a quarter mile from where my parents lived. The tracks were in the woods behind the house. I photographed them and sent the pictures to the *Chronicle*, which promptly lost them—along with the negatives. The weird thing about the tracks, as I recall, is that there were only three of them, and they seemed to end suddenly in the snow.

It was in that same month that my grandmother, one of the kindest and wisest people I've ever known, looked out of her window that chilly morning and saw what seemed to be a very large creature "all curled up" on her lawn, seemingly resting there.

Much later, she told me, "I didn't tell anyone because I was afraid people would cart me away somewhere. It was only afterward, when other people said they had seen the same things, that I talked about it."

My grandmother related her experience to me:

There was some big black thing all curled up down at the end of the lawn one morning, when I got up really bright and early. And then I saw tracks [in the snow] and I never said a word because I thought they were going to say, "She's nutty."

I had my garbage in a green bag, the same as I have on the back porch now, only I had it out here by the corner of the house and it used to be [around this time] taken up and set down in the lawn down there, and things were taken out of it.

The bag wasn't torn. But the food was taken out, and just as though a person took it out or something—nothing like an animal would do, and I kept wondering about that because if the dogs get in it . . . it's all over the place, and this wasn't. It was very neat.

And my neighbor over here called me after that and she said her garbage that she had in a shed had had the same thing done to it. And she . . . found the empty bag in a tree . . . It was just picked up out of the shed and carried away.

My grandmother was seventy-two at the time of these events, and sharp as a tack, just as she was up until she passed away at the age of eighty-seven in 1993. She didn't get a good look at the creature on her lawn, as dawn was just breaking, but she attempted to describe it to me: "I think it had quite long hair. And it was very tall. It was sort of circled, curled up."

Interestingly enough, the "wild man" of Russian lore, known as "alma," also supposedly rests in a curled-up position, according to eyewitnesses. My grandmother further described her sighting: "The one funny thing about that creature, whatever it is, it seems to appear and disappear. One minute it's there and the next minute it's gone. And we have seen tracks leading somewhere and even the tracks seem to stop right there, and you don't see them anymore. That's a mystery. The whole thing is a mystery to me."

Tracks that my father thought may have belonged to a bear were seen all that winter. He also made another very intriguing discovery: three dead rabbits stuffed into the snow at the top of Cushing's Hill. It was as though they had been placed there for winter storage by whatever had killed them. Curiously, there were no tracks found nearby, nor was there any sign of blood.

It was a year later—December 5, 1979, to be precise—that my cousin Barry saw something near Cushing's Hill that truly frightened him. My grandmother later described the incident to researchers Robert and Paul Bartholomew and William Brann: "My grandson Barry was setting traps one day and he came back and his face was so white—as white as could be—and he said to me, 'Grandma, I saw four great big things crossing the creek and going into the woods down there.' And I'm sure he saw something because I hadn't mentioned anything I'd seen before that. And then I told everyone that I had seen the tracks before."

Barry described what he had seen to both my grandmother and me: four light brown, furry creatures that walked on two legs, striding through the water to cross the creek, making "clacking and grunting" sounds as they went. Though the brush made them difficult to see, he was sure they were larger than he was—and even at age fourteen, Barry was about six feet tall.

A few months later, in April 1980, a woman who wanted to be identified only as "Barbara" had an extraordinary sighting as she was driving home from work one night on Route 9. She had just crossed the county line from Rensselaer County into Columbia County; on her right were fairly dense woods and on her left was an unplanted cornfield.

In her car's headlights, she saw something that she couldn't believe she was seeing. She later described it to me as something about seven and a half feet tall, with reddish-brown hair or fur. In her words, "It looked like a highly evolved ape." Barbara slowed down her car to get a better look and stared at the huge creature as it walked across the road and into the cornfield. It then disappeared into the darkness. She didn't report her sighting until nearly a year later.

I once heard something that I am now convinced was a vocalization made by one of these creatures. In July 1980, I was escorting a friend who was visiting from England back to the place where she was staying. It was about eleven o'clock at night and the moon was full as we stepped off of my grandparents' front porch. Then, from the depths of the forest behind the house, we heard the most frightening sound I have ever heard in my life. There was no question that it was the vocalization of some large animal: it began with a series of grunting noises, and then turned into a series of screaming or screeching sounds, ultimately dying out in a kind of low moan. It must have lasted for all of thirty seconds.

After a moment of stunned silence, my friend turned to me and said matter-of-factly, "Is that a typical American sound to hear at night?"

I told her that no, it was not, and that I had never heard anything like it before. I wish I had possessed the presence of mind to investigate whatever it was that had made that sound. At the time, I was still somewhat skeptical that bigfoot, or whatever one likes to call it, was roaming Columbia County. In any case, I didn't think my friend would want to look into what might have made that unearthly din, so I didn't press the issue. I look back at this incident now as a case of missed opportunity.

The night of September 24, 1980, was one I will never forget. That was the night that I became convinced there was some unknown creature roaming the area. There was a huge "hunter's moon" that evening and my cousin Barry and I decided to take a walk around the golf course that was just up the road from my grandparents' house. Ironically, we were making fun of the whole bigfoot controversy; Barry was trying to rationalize what he had seen a couple of years previously. We said something to the effect of, "Okay, bigfoot, come out and put up your dukes."

Much to our surprise, that was exactly what happened later that night. That year was one of the few in which I kept a daily diary. My entry for September 24 read: "Incredible day. Walked around the golf course in the afternoon and had the weirdest sensation of being followed by something, but could see nothing unusual. Later, Barry and I walked around the golf course again and heard all the dogs barking their heads off. Went out to Chatham at about nine p.m., was called by my grandmother who wanted me to come home because there was a 'something' outside the house terrifying her. By the time I got home, it was gone."

Between 11:00 and 11:45 that evening, my aunt Barbara (Barry's mother) had brought my grandmother home from her house in the Village of Kinderhook. Accompanying her in the car were Barbara's daughter Chari and Chari's six-month-old daughter, Melanie. My aunt was getting out of the car with my grandmother to carry some water jugs into the house when they heard alarming vocalizations from only a few feet away, around the corner of the root cellar.

My grandmother said to Barbara, "What in the world was that?" Barbara didn't reply; she just stood there frozen. The screams and groans continued from around the corner of the root cellar. Chari, who had stayed in the car with her baby, screamed, "Get in the car, Mom!" when she heard the sounds—then, in panic, locked all the doors before her mother could get into the car. She quickly realized her mistake and unlocked the doors.

As the terrifying sounds continued, Barbara decided she would go and get her son to come over with his shotgun. My grandfather was away at the time, so Barry was the only one in the family with a gun at the moment.

For whatever reason, my grandmother said she would wait in the house while Barbara went to get Barry. She was alone there, and that was when she had called me. She sat in her living-room chair, armed with a hammer. She later recalled, "When she [Barbara] backed out of the driveway, the thing went down below the hill and it just moaned—oh, the most terrible moan and groan—until the car lights were back in the driveway. Then it came right back up here again and made all those noises again, until he [Barry] got his gun."

When Barry arrived, he heard the screams from just around the corner of the root cellar. He fired his shotgun three times to scare off the intruder—or intruders. "I'm sure there were two of them," my grandmother said later, "because, by our pine tree out here, there was one making the same noise. Well, when [Barry] shot, it just screamed, and this one by the back door, I could see the shadow of this terrible great big thing. Oh, my goodness, that was the worst thing.

"It wasn't until he fired the third time that the thing screamed and ran off. That time, flame came out of the shotgun."

When I came home that night, all of those events had already transpired. I had just missed all the excitement, but my skepticism toward local bigfoot reports was gone. My grandmother had never been one to be afraid of anything; I remember one day when she chased three hunters with rifles out of her backyard—with a broom!

But this thing, whatever it was, had gotten to her. My mother and father lived less than a mile away from my grandparents, and my mother—who was alone that night because my father and grandfather had gone camping in the Adirondacks—had heard the shots fired and later found out all that had happened that wild night. She wrote a letter to *Albany Times Union* columnist Barney Fowler, a nature and sports writer who subsequently wrote a feature titled "Mystery 'Creature' of Kinderhook" a few days after the incident. The feature read, in part:

> No idle talk this: folks in the Town of Kinderhook have been hearing from and seeing some strange things. This from a family in the area:
>
> "Last Wednesday my mother-in-law, now in her seventies, who lives a quarter mile up the road from us, came home around ten-thirty PM and around the back of the house came this horrible scream. She was terrified; it screamed, moaned, made guttural noises, and finally my nephew got his gun and fired into the air. It moved away, walking on TWO legs, such as a human would do.
>
> "Also, we have seen large footprints in the snow and my husband thought perhaps it might be a bear . . . Do you or anyone have any idea what this thing could be? On talking to other people in the area, they have heard it too."

Fowler ended his article by making a request: "I'd be interested in hearing other comments on the creature." They were not long in coming. A man from nearby New Lebanon wrote that he had heard the same vocalizations "on a foggy, humid night in the woods." Dr. Gary Levine, a social sciences professor and paranormal investigator from Columbia-Greene Community College, proposed "a psychic look at the creature."

Meanwhile, a schoolteacher on Hennett Road, a mile or so from my grandparents' home, claimed to have heard the vocalizations. Fowler's column was packed with such stories right through Halloween that year, at which point, he wrote to his readers, "Maybe we've gone overboard on this thing."

That was pretty much the end of bigfoot reports in Fowler's column. Yet, whether they were the subject of media stories or not, the sightings in Columbia County continued. In November 1980, two of my cousins told me they had been walking up Novak Road in the vicinity of Cushing's Hill when they heard the sound of something large moving through the woods on both sides of the road. It was a dark night with a crescent moon, but they were able to make out five figures converging in the road in front of them. The figures were very tall and they seemed to have no necks and rather conical heads.

My cousin's girlfriend corroborated this sighting in a fascinating way: she had been on the way to meet him when she saw an immense bipedal creature reaching into the trash can near her house, pulling out food and consuming it. She had her small dog with her, and it became highly agitated, barking its head off and urinating in the road. My cousins never met up with her that night; they had taken off in fright in the other direction.

Members of my family continued to have encounters with these creatures. My cousin Chari saw something in November 1981 that she described as a "big two-legged thing, reddish-brown, that ran off into the woods" that had walked in front of her car on a chilly night. She was quite shaken up by the incident, as it had occurred very near my grandparents' home.

Mike Maab, a retired employee of the Ichabod Crane Central School District, was fishing late one afternoon in May 1982 at the Kinderhook Creek when he looked up and saw something observing him from the other side of the creek from around twenty yards away. Maab described the creature as about eight feet tall, with long hair on its head and short hair of a reddish-brown color on its body. He also noted that it had small red eyes and, in the sunlight, he could even see that its fingernails were black. He and the creature stared at each other for a few moments, and Maab had the impression the creature was as curious about him as he was about it. Then the thing simply walked off into the woods and he didn't see it again.

After the syndicated television show *PM Magazine* came to do a story on what they dubbed "The Kinderhook Creature," I began to receive reports from people all over Columbia County who claimed to have seen such things. Two hunters near Austerlitz, a hamlet about eight miles from Kinderhook, said they had been hunting in the nearby Berkshire Hills when one of them encountered an eight-foot-tall creature. It so terrified the man that he dropped his rifle and ran until his friend caught up with him and tried to get him to go back into the woods and retrieve his gun. He refused, and his friend had to go and get it for him. The hunter who had seen the creature emphasized, "No way it could be a bear."

In 1982, during the autumn apple season (a very big deal in these parts), there were a number of sightings of a "white Bigfoot" reported in and near some of the apple orchards. One had been seen running through an orchard at great speed.

Perhaps the strangest sighting of that time came from a woman named Margaret Mayer, who was interviewed by Robert Bartholomew and me on June 15, 1985. The previous night, Mayer had been driving on Route 203 near the Winding Brook Golf Course when she saw a strange creature standing on the left side of the road. She related, "The first thing I noticed was the eyes. I sort of thought it was a deer. The eyes were down almost level with the road at first. Then it sort of stood up . . . It was like four or five feet taller than when I first saw it. It stood there for a little while, and it looked across the road, looking in my direction."

She emphasized: "It wasn't a person . . . The eyes were sort of small . . . but very far apart. It looked straight at me a couple of times. It only moved from the top part of its shoulders and the head. I didn't notice any arms. I could see the top of the legs, but the odd thing was, they were really skinny . . . It looked . . . deformed. That's why I was surprised it could move so fast. It didn't seem to walk across the road. It seemed a smoother type of movement . . . almost gliding . . . The eyes were yellow . . . and the head went straight into the shoulders . . . no neck."

When I look back on these events now, they almost seem like dreams, or perhaps scenes out of a monster movie. And yet these things really happened. At first, my grandmother was frightened of the creature, but in later years she said to me, "I wish it would come around again. It was so exciting!"

In May 1993, on the day before she died, my grandmother was interviewed by a local newspaper about her sightings, and she told the same story she had told dozens of times, without varying on any detail. She died peacefully in the wee small hours of the following morning.

Reports have died down since the eighties, although there are occasional rumors of tracks being found and strange vocalizations in the woods of Columbia County. Perhaps the creatures have moved on, migrating to a more remote area. My only regret is that I didn't get to see them while they were here. It was an extraordinary, incredible time that will never come again.

Alligators in the Sewers, Giant Rats, and Other Urban Legends

rban legends have lives of their own. They usually begin with someone—generally, but not always, a teenager—saying something like, "My friend John knows someone who knows someone" or, "I read somewhere that . . ." Most urban legends are just that, legends. But there are some that have a basis in fact, and perhaps surprisingly to many readers, the tales of alligators in the New York City sewers have much more than a grain of truth to them.

Most accounts agree that the story of the "Sewer Gator" began in the 1930s. According to cryptozoologist Loren Coleman in his book *Mysterious America*, "swarms" of alligators were seen in the Bronx River in 1932 and one that measured three feet long was found dead. On March 7, 1935, another three-foot gator was caught alive in Yonkers. Two years later, on June 1, 1937, a barge captain on the East River captured a four-footer. Five days later, a city resident caught a two-foot gator at the subway entrance to the Brooklyn Museum.

Perhaps the most credible Sewer Gator report, however, appeared in the February 10, 1935 edition of the *New York Times*. The headline read: "Alligator Found In Uptown Sewer . . . Whence It Came Is Mystery." The story told of an extraordinary encounter between sixteen-year-old Salvatore Condolucci, a few of his friends, and an alligator they found frolicking near a sewer entrance where they were throwing snowballs and slush. Condolucci was the first to see the alligator in the sewer below, but eventually his friends Frank Lonzo and Jimmy Mireno confirmed that he was not hallucinating: there really was a gator down there, and it was big.

Apparently, the beast was thrashing about in the ice, trying to get free of it. The boys decided to help it in its quest and promptly fetched some clothesline, which one of them tied into a slip knot and dangled over the reptile. Eventually, the boys looped it around the neck of the creature and together they pulled the gator from the ice and up to the street, where it just lay there, sluggish from the cold.

When one of the youths tried to loosen the rope, the gator woke up and snapped its jaws at him. The boys then realized they may have made a mistake in bringing the alligator to the street of a great metropolis; their "sympathy turned to enmity," according to the article, and they used their snow shovels to kill the beast, which was already weakened.

They then dragged their "victim" to the Lehigh Stove and Repair Shop, where the startled shop owner found the creature to weigh 125 pounds and to be seven-and-a-half to eight feet in length. By this time, most of the surrounding neighborhood had seen the gator being dragged through the streets and into the shop, and a crowd had gathered. Someone called the police, but there wasn't much they could do at this point. As the article noted, "The strange visitor was quite dead; and no charge could be preferred against it or its slayers. The neighbors were calmed with little trouble and speculation as to where the 'gator came from was rife."

The theory that it might have escaped from a pet shop was ruled out almost immediately; there were no pet shops in the area. "Finally," according to the feature, "the theories simmered down to that of a passing boat. Plainly, a steamer from the mysterious Everglades, or thereabouts, had been passing 123rd Street, and the alligator had fallen overboard."

Needless to say, that theory was never proven either, and the startling newspaper story ended on this rather sad note: "At about nine p.m., when tired mothers had succeeded in getting most of their alligator-conscious youngsters to bed, a Department of Sanitation truck rumbled up to the store and made off with the prize. Its destination was Barren Island and an incinerator."

That one newspaper item from one of the country's most respected dailies is proof that the stories of the so-called Sewer Gators are no mere myths. The rumors were given additional weight by two books that were published much later: Robert Daley's *The World Beneath the City* (1959) and Thomas Pynchon's first novel, *V* (1963). Daley's book was a history of the development of the utilities network on Manhattan Island. One chapter of the book is actually titled "Alligators in the Sewers," and arose from a series of interviews with Teddy May, the former commissioner of sewers in New York.

May told Daley that he had first heard rumors of alligators from various sewer inspectors in 1935, but that he did not believe them at the time. In fact, he suspected that the inspectors reporting these rumors may have been drinking on the job, so he hired some extra men to spy on them and let him know how they were smuggling their liquor down into the sewers.

The reports continued, however, and when the article about the gator appeared in the *New York Times*, May decided to go down into the sewers and take a look for himself. According to Daley, he discovered that the inspectors were, indeed, not drinking, and that the reports were true: "The beam of his own flashlight had spotlighted alligators whose length, on the average, was about two feet," wrote Daley.

According to May, the gators had avoided the dangerously swift currents of the main sewer lines by hiding out near the smaller pipes in the less-traveled areas of the city, what Loren Coleman colorfully called "the backwash." May decided that, as the alligators had apparently settled in, it was his duty to get rid of them.

Rat poison was used to dispose of some of them. Others were forced into the fast currents, which quickly drowned them or washed them out to sea. Some were hunted down by armed sewer inspectors "on their own free time." By 1937, May announced to the public that he and his department had rid New York City of its alligator problem.

Apparently, however, his announcement was premature. In 1938, five alligators were captured in New Rochelle, New York, and more sightings of sewer gators were reported in 1948 and 1966. Pynchon's novel *V* fictionalized these events, positing that the alligators came originally from Macy's Department Store, where baby alligators were sold for fifty cents, mainly to children. Unfortunately, the children became bored with them—baby alligators don't do much in captivity, including eat, which makes them rather dull pets—so, according to Pynchon's book, the children set them loose in the streets, as well as flushed them down the toilets to get rid of them. Armed citizens with shotguns got rid of them in *V* and one of the book's characters, Benny Profane, hunted alligators as a full-time occupation.

In some variations on the rumors, it's postulated that, because alligators were flushed into the sewers at such a young age, they would live mainly in the dark and in time would lose their eyesight and their coloring. In other words, they would become albinos. No "official" reports of albino alligator sightings have ever been posted, however. Most herpetologists believe that alligators would not be able to survive and reproduce in the sewers, despite the fact that the environment is fairly warm and stable year round.

As always in the field of cryptozoology, though, skepticism doesn't keep reports from coming in. And, in rare cases, these reports can be confirmed by a mere excursion to the zoo. In June 2001, several people reported they had seen a small alligator in a pond in Central Park near a sewage drain. Although these reports were at first assumed to be hoaxes, the city sent in a crew to check the storm drain just to be on the safe side, and they did indeed find a caiman alligator a couple feet long. It was transported to the children's zoo in Central Park where it is still on exhibit today. No explanation was offered as to how a South American caiman ended up in Central Park.

Apparently, sewer alligators are not the only cryptids on the loose beneath the streets of New York. Immense rats have been reported for years in New York City's subway system and in other areas in and under the city. In 2011, the *New York Daily News* reported that large rats were "invading New York," and proof arrived shortly after via a photograph published in that newspaper showing a man with a dead rat on the end of his pitchfork. Housing Authority worker Jose Rivera had speared the giant rodent at a Brooklyn housing project called the Marcy Houses. Rivera told the *Daily News*: "I hit it one time and it was still moving . . . I hit it another time and that's when it died. I'm not scared of rats but I was scared of being bitten."

The rat in question was three feet long and weighed more than two pounds, the size of a small dog. Unnamed sources claimed they had seen as many as eight huge rats killed at one time around the same building and on an adjoining playground. Experts identified the rat killed by Rivera as a Gambian pouched rat, a species sometimes kept as pets. As the

Daily News noted, however, "that doesn't make it any less terrifying."

A woman on the subway on June 10, 2012, was certainly terrified when, in the middle of a packed rush-hour train, a large rat ran up her trouser leg. According to the *Daily News* article, "Ana Vargas, forty, was sitting in the train at 7:50 a.m. as it approached New York's Columbus Circle station when the terrifying rodent crawled up her leg . . . Despite violently shaking her trousers, the large rodent still didn't drop out."

Vargas was forced to pull her pants down in front of the other passengers to get rid of the rat: "I grabbed his head, because he was scratching me . . . I didn't want it to bite," she told the *Daily News*. Three gentlemen shielded her from "flashing" people on the train and, as the train pulled up to its destination, she was able to drop the rat "and ran for help in a state of shock." The article claimed that, "Following the rat attack, extra inspections have been carried out on the subway network."

Unlike alligators, rats of any size have no problems living and breeding in sewers and subways. These scavengers can live off food from trash bins. And, as photographs have proven, they sometimes achieve alarming size.

Moving up from sewers and subways for a moment, we find that downstate New York had its own bigfoot scares in the early years of the twentieth century. Long Island was the perhaps improbable setting for these incidents, which began in February 1909 when residents of Patchogue, Eastport, Quogue, and Westhampton reported sighting a frightening creature that uttered a "blood-curdling shriek." The nocturnal beast was said to "glare out of the thickets with eyes of flame." Some of those who glimpsed the animal described it as "monkey-like" or resembling a "baboon."

Some Westhampton residents theorized that the creature must "have come ashore on the wreckage of a deep bark" and "to have taken to the woods." The *New York Herald* reported in its February 7, 1909, edition, "Strong men with guns (went) into the forests at dead of night to find the thing, be it bird or devil, panther or baboon." Needless to say, the elusive creature was never found.

Thirteen years later it was back, when in early November 1922, a "ferocious baboon in the wilds of Long Island" was reported near Babylon. Again, search parties were sent out and came back with nothing, and the creature was described either as a "baboon" or a "gorilla."

In 1931, another flap began when sightings of a "wandering gorilla or perhaps a chimpanzee" were reported in the vicinity of Huntington. Described as an "apelike . . . hairy creature, about four feet tall," it was initially seen in June near Mineola, by six people at a child-care nursery. Armed police made a search, but again found nothing. No animals had been reported missing from nearby zoos either. By the end of June, several armed police units had been formed to find the beast, but all they were able to come up with were footprints about the size of a man's hand, which seemed to suggest a two-legged creature.

On July 18, a nursery employee saw the creature walking through some shrubbery, while a nearby farmer claimed to have seen a similarly "strange animal." Investigating police again found footprints at both sites, but lost the trail in the tangled brush. In Amityville—a name now synonymous with hauntings and an alleged demonic possession—reports of "an eight-foot-tall gorilla with glowing red eyes" started coming in. On September 5, 1934, the headline in the *New York Herald Tribune* shouted: "Man, Beast or Demon? It's Loose in Amityville." The article read, in part: "The mysterious animal, described by some as a large monkey . . . paid a visit early this morning to the home of Mrs. Alfred C. Abernathy, of Bennett Place, South Amityville, tore up an old fur coat, ripped several mattresses and clawed an old automobile in the garage. Tonight most of the male residents of the neighborhood are sitting on their porches waiting for the animal with shotguns, rifles, revolvers and garden hoses."

The creature was never found and the sightings on Long Island have never been explained. Were they connected with later bigfoot sightings that were reported upstate? Or was "an eight-foot gorilla with glowing red eyes" something demonic, as befits the famous Amityville haunting? We may never know the answer.

From Long Island, we travel to nearby Staten Island, a densely populated parcel of land that hardly seems a proper home for some unlikely creature. And yet, beginning in the 1970s, reports of a bigfoot-like creature have not been uncommon on the island. According to the book *Weird New York* by Chris Gethard, a December 1974 report filed by two Staten Islanders walking in a wooded area at Historic Richmond Town told of meeting "face to face with a monstrous beast covered from head to toe in brown hair."

On January 21, 1975, a couple saw the same (or similar) creature striding across a church parking lot. That very night, a woman nearly hit the beast with her car as it emerged from that same parking lot and ran across the road and into a nearby landfill.

There have been sporadic sightings of this creature or creatures since then, including one as recently as 2002. According to Gethard, the theory among the locals is that the Staten Island Bigfoot—for want of a better term—"spends most of its time somewhere in the Greenbelt, a nature preserve consisting of 2,800 acres of dense forest."

Kent is a small town in Putnam County that is home to something called "The Ford Street Beast." According to Tim Davis, a contributor to the book *Weird New York*, Ford Street is a short road "no longer than a football field." Davis described the Ford Street Beast as "around six to seven feet tall, having dark fur and a doglike face that seems to sit directly on its shoulders as if it has no neck at all," according to eyewitnesses. One witness claimed that it ran in front of his car, and that it has the ability to run on all four legs "much like a large feline," but that it stands on two legs "when it feels threatened." The beast may perhaps be a paranormal entity, for Davis concluded his short but tantalizing entry with this statement: "People say they usually see it only at night, and when they do, it sometimes disappears as a cloud of vapor or dust."

The Montauk Monster
and
Other Mysteries

Twenty-six-year-old Jenna Hewitt of Montauk, Long Island, and three of her friends were walking on the beach on July 12, 2008, when they saw something that startled them: the carcass of a strange beast. Hewitt later told the local newspaper, *The Independent*: "We were looking for a place to sit when we saw some people looking at something . . . We didn't know what it was."

The beach, a popular surfing spot at Rheinstein Estate Park in East Hampton, was an unlikely location to see such a creature, alive or dead. It looked like some sort of huge rodent with a beak like that of a dinosaur, a four-pawed thing lying on its belly in the sand. Its lower jaw appeared to have a set of jagged teeth, while its upper jaw sported that bony beak. The body was "stocky and robust," as zoologist Darren Naish pointed out on scienceblogs.com. The limbs, however, were slender, while the digits on its "hands" were long, with pale-colored claws. The slim tail was "about equal in length to the head and neck combined," noted Naish.

The feature published in *The Independent* on July 23, 2008, was titled "The Hound of Bonacville," referring to Sir Arthur Conan Doyle's famous novel *The Hound of the Baskervilles* as well as to the local name "Bonackers," a term for the natives of East Hampton. The article by Kitty Merrill was somewhat tongue-in-cheek, but noted, "Imaginations did run a little wild last week after the corpse . . . was found on the beach above the high tide line in Montauk . . . Some who saw it thought it might be a turtle sans shell, while others wondered whether it wasn't an escaped mutant victim of diabolical experiments taken by the sea from Plum Island. It looked like it had a beak and molars and (shudder) human hands!

"A less fanciful observer speculated it was a raccoon someone killed and skinned—a portion of the remaining fur on one leg appears to have been pulled down. That one was the closest conjecture confirmed by experts . . . Prior to contact from this paper, no other local agencies were alerted to the grisly discovery. According to a member of the crowd of gawkers that gathered around the fly-riddled carcass, someone took it away . . . to be buried."

Once Hewitt's photograph appeared in the newspaper, it quickly circulated through other papers and the Internet. The mystery of what happened to the body deepened when Hewitt claimed that "a guy took it and put it in the woods in his back yard," but she would not identify the person nor say exactly where he took it. Hewitt's father went on record denying that Hewitt was keeping the location of the carcass a secret.

Hewitt and her friends suddenly found themselves local celebrities, appearing on *Plum-TV*, a public-access TV show in Montauk. Popular website Gawker.com obtained Hewitt's photo and posted it on July 29, under the headline "Dead Monster Washes Ashore in Montauk." The national media picked up on the story and the "monster" even made a guest appearance on an episode of the History Channel's *Ancient Aliens* television series, despite the fact that no one was claiming the thing to be a space alien.

Hewitt noted to the media, "We joked that maybe it [the "monster"] was something from Plum Island." And that's where the mystery deepens further still.

The Plum Island Animal Disease Center of New York, as it is officially known, is a federal facility whose public goal is to study diseases that afflict animals. At the height of the Cold War in the 1950s, a secret biological weapons program targeting livestock was conducted at Plum Island, which is one of the main reasons that the facility remains shrouded in mystery and controversy. Many people may have first heard of Plum Island from the 1991 film *Silence of the Lambs*, in which Hannibal Lecter, played by Anthony Hopkins, refers to the place as "Anthrax Island."

Plum Island is actually located off the coast of Connecticut, although it is considered to be part of New York State. The island was purchased by the U.S. government during the Spanish-American War, during which time the army erected Fort Terry. Today, the island's Animal Disease Center includes seventy buildings, many of which are now quite run-down, on 840 acres of land. The island has its own fire department, power plant, and water treatment plant, and any wild mammal that is seen on the island is killed on sight.

In 1992, the facility was opened to the media for the first time, and three years later, the Department of Agriculture was forced to pay an $111,000 fine for storing hazardous chemicals on the island. In 2002, the *Wall Street Journal* published a piece noting that numerous scientists and government authorities wanted the laboratory to close due to these controversies, and also due to the fact that foot-and-mouth disease, which the facility had originally been developed to fight, was an unlikely threat to warrant the lab's $16.5 million yearly budget.

The most controversial site on the island is Building 257, which is located in the original Fort Terry and was built in 1911. Originally, the building was used to store weapons and was called the Combined Torpedo Storehouse and Cable Tanks building. The United States Army Chemical Corps took over the facility in 1952 and used it for biological warfare research, which involved the remodeling of Building 257 and several other sites.

In 2004, attorney Michael Carroll published a book called *Lab 257: The Disturbing Story of the Government's Secret Plum Island Germ Laboratory.* Among other claims, Carroll's book asserts that Lyme Disease was the result of experiments made at Plum Island. Although David Weld, director of the American Lyme Disease Foundation, has said that he doesn't think that claim has any merit, he has refused to speculate on how many birds that roost and nest on the island fly back and forth to the mainland—birds that may carry infected ticks.

Plum Island is also the subject of a mystery novel called, simply enough, *Plum Island*, by famed crime novelist Nelson DeMille. The book concerns an investigation of the murder of two scientists who worked on the island.

It was this sinister background that gave rise to the theory that the Montauk Monster had been the result of some sort of biological experiment on Plum Island. The location where the carcass was found matched where something from the island may have turned up when considering the currents and the island's proximity to the mainland. Although zoologist Naish and East Hampton Natural Resources Director Larry Penny opined that, based on the photograph—which was all that remained for them to study—the "monster" may have been a dead raccoon that had been buffeted by the tides and partially decomposed, others claim that the creature was some type of hybrid biological monster, perhaps part bird, part canine.

There is yet another mystery surrounding Montauk that, some say, could be the source of mysterious creatures.

Certainly, the "high strangeness" factor surrounding the so-called "Montauk Project" could, if true, yield some very bizarre things indeed.

Rumors about the Montauk Project have been circulating since the early 1980s. The project was allegedly a series of top-secret U.S. government experiments conducted at, depending upon the source, either Camp Hero, a military base in Montauk that was decommissioned in 1981, or at Montauk Air Force Station. The experiments supposedly had to do with exotic research such as time travel and psychological warfare techniques. UFO researcher Jacques Vallee feels that these rumors arose out of stories about the Philadelphia Experiment, supposed to have been conducted at the Philadelphia Naval Shipyard in 1943. During that project, a Navy destroyer was allegedly rendered invisible to enemy radar and other devices.

According to the story, the USS *Eldridge* was bombarded with electromagnetic energy and became invisible to radar; it also became literally invisible, apparently due to teleportation. Supposedly, for a few seconds, the ship materialized off the coast of Norfolk, Virginia, more than two hundred miles away. It was further claimed that the USS *Eldridge* sat for some time in plain view of the men aboard the ship SS *Andrew Furuseth*, then vanished from their sight and reappeared in Philadelphia at the site where it had originally been docked. It was also said that the ship traveled approximately ten seconds in time.

The experiment was claimed to have been based on an aspect of Einstein's unified field theory, which unites the fields of electromagnetism and gravity into one field. According to the theory, if light was bent, then space-time would be as well, creating an "invisible time machine."

Several of the crew members of the USS *Eldridge* were said to have died horrible, bizarre deaths as a result of the experiment. The October experiment was allegedly the second try; on the first attempt during the summer of 1943, the ship was rendered nearly invisible, with some witnesses claiming to have seen a "greenish fog" appearing in its place. Once the ship returned from whatever strange realm it went into, crew members complained of severe nausea—but that was not all. The story goes that when the ship reappeared, some of the crew were embedded in the metal structures of the ship, their flesh having fused together with the ship's metal during the "teleportation." One sailor supposedly ended up on a lower deck level than where he had begun, and his hand was embedded in the steel hull of the ship. Some sailors were said to have gone "completely bananas," according to one witness who was interviewed many years later on the History Channel.

After these bizarre experiments, scientists and military officials wanted to continue their research, but not in such a highly visible place as the Philadelphia Naval Shipyard. At that time, Montauk was a quiet and sparsely populated area, and it was allegedly deemed to be the perfect spot to carry out further experiments. Although situated at the tip of Long Island, it was still fairly close to New York City, which appealed to the shadowy individuals behind the top-secret project.

Sometime during the fifties, it is said, construction started on a vast subterranean complex that would house the military and scientific personnel behind the project. According to the story, the base went into operation in the early sixties, and by the seventies, the experiments being conducted under the streets of Montauk had become the stuff of legend.

According to most sources, the focus of the Montauk Project was on mind control as well as the continuation of work on "electromagnetic shielding" and time travel. Young men with alleged psychic sensitivity were brought to the underground labs and seated in a chair that was developed to enhance their latent ESP. The chair was supposedly blasted with energy waves that allowed the researchers to control their subjects' thoughts. The story goes that the most adept of these psychics were able to focus on imagined objects to such a degree that the objects would actually materialize physically, if only for a few moments.

The star psychic of these experiments was said to be a man named Duncan Cameron. He supposedly had the ability to manipulate not only space, but time as well. At this juncture, some officials involved in the project felt that it had gone too far and was spiraling out of control. The stories got wilder and wilder: allegedly wormholes were being created on the base for the purposes of time travel, and the fear was that civilians living in Montauk above the facility may have been endangered.

In August 1983, the project allegedly came to a frightening end. The officials in charge of the project proposed to travel exactly forty years into the past to connect with their predecessors aboard the USS *Eldridge* in Philadelphia. Some of the scientists involved who wanted to end the project decided on a novel way to do it: they got Duncan Cameron to visualize a large, angry, and powerful creature that looked something like a bigfoot. Cameron supposedly brought this mind-projection (known as a "tulpa") to physical life, whereupon the beast began to destroy the facilities in some sort of monstrous rage. The legend says that this beast completely destroyed the labs, disconnecting the project from its travels to the past and destroying the equipment that harnessed psychic power.

Once this destructive feat was accomplished, the creature dematerialized and the scientists' "time tunnels" collapsed; the project was forever ended and the base was closed and left to deteriorate. Some of the witnesses to what had occurred were allegedly brainwashed and made to forget what they had seen. Others swore never to reveal what had happened there.

Montauk Air Force Station was closed and the site was reopened to the public in 2002 as Camp Hero State Park. The U.S. military, however, still owns the property underneath the park. Tales are told that military officials still patrol the area. To this day, rumors circulate on the Internet that a project connected to Montauk is still operational beneath the Rome National Air Base in Rome, New York, several hundred miles upstate. According to these rumors, scientists in underground facilities there are using what is called the "Montauk Chair" to conduct psychic experiments similar to what was done in Montauk.

If one takes these admittedly wild, unsubstantiated stories at face value, they could explain a lot. Here are some "what ifs": What if some of the bigfoot sightings in fairly heavily populated regions of New York State aren't of living beings at all, but rather of tulpas created by thought projection? What if the Montauk Monster, rather than being the result of an experiment at Plum Island, was instead the result of a teleportation experiment gone wrong, thereby explaining its seemingly contradictory features of both mammal and bird? And what if any number of bizarre creatures that have been seen over the years were somehow connected to the Montauk Project?

Take the Sasquatch of Central Park, for instance. A 2009 article posted on mania.com by paranormal investigator Nick Redfern was titled "Lair of the Beasts: A New York Monster." Redfern tells of a case that was reported to him by a man known only as "Barry" of an event that happened in Central Park. An assistant manager at a hotel that overlooked the park, Barry told Redfern that on a sunny weekday in the summer of 1997, he was strolling through the park on his lunch break. All seemed normal until he approached a somewhat brushy spot and an unknown animal burst through the brush.

Redfern wrote, "Barry claimed to me that the creature was man-like in shape and covered in hair of a distinctly rusty color—but, unlike the towering Bigfoot of the west coast, was little more than three feet in height. Little-Foot might have been a far better term to use."

Barry watched "with a mixture of shock and awe" as the midget-sized man-beast "charged across the path in front of him at a distance of no more than about twenty feet, came to a screeching halt for a couple of seconds to stare intently into his eyes, and then headed off at high speed again, before finally vanishing; beneath a small bridge inside the perimeter of the park, no less."

A bridge troll? No wonder Barry was embarrassed about discussing his sighting with Redfern, even through e-mail and twelve years removed from the incident. As Redfern concluded, "Barry's was just one of those very odd, fringe cases that seem to really perplex from time to time those of us who dare to dig into the world of monsters and strange creatures."

Another "fringe case" came from the town of Sherman, New York, as reported by author John Keel in his book, *The Complete Guide to Mysterious Beings*. Keel received a letter in 1970 from an unidentified teenage resident of Sherman. In his letter to Keel, the teen reported that he had seen two gigantic, white, slothlike creatures visit his parents' swampland property between 1965 and 1970. Keel quoted the young man in his book: "I am writing because about three or four years ago, I saw a white monster in a swamp beside our house. I have been seeing these things ever since and close to our house. One night it came down in our yard."

The young man described the creature(s) as follows: "It stands between twelve and eighteen feet high, it has a long tail between six and eight feet long. It is all covered with hair. They are always white. I have seen them alone or two at a time. It can walk on two feet or four feet. It is almost a double for a Prehistoric Sloth. My whole family has seen this thing and I know of two more men who have seen them . . . I am fifteen years old and I am not kidding. I have seen these things and they are real."

This is the only known report of such strange, slothlike creatures that has ever been recorded. The identity of the teenager who reported the story has never been confirmed. Perhaps a trip by some enterprising cryptozoologist to the swamps in Sherman, at the western edge of New York State, might be in order.

Meanwhile, there are plenty of other weirdies waiting to be discovered. Back in Long Island, there was a report to the "Phantoms and Monsters" blog from a woman identified only as "Jeni," regarding a truly strange cryptid she had witnessed. In her post on the blog, she noted that she grew up on Long Island and was familiar with the Montauk Project and Brookhaven Labs. She claimed that one moonlit night in 2006, she and her fiancé witnessed a bizarre creature on a beach near Hampton Bay: "It appeared translucent/transparent," she wrote. "This 'creature' was shaped and moving in the way a Manta Ray would; yet completely transparent! No color at all; I could see the stars through this thing . . . It was larger than a standard sedan. Its wingspan was at least, from what I could estimate, ten feet in width; while it was "flying," its wings moved up and down . . . It was approximately ten to fifteen feet over my head; it had no visible head or tail; no discernible limbs or appendages of any kind." Jeni wrote that after a few seconds of staring at the bizarre beast, she and her fiancé ran to their car and never looked back.

There was more, however: "We started heading back on Dune Road when we saw what I could only describe as two smaller 'rays' which moved more like a bat would, flying together from right to left overhead past the car. These two were translucent and had a grayish color to them."

Now we travel full circle to come back to the Montauk Monster, or something very similar. A young man from Northville in Sussex County on Long Island discovered the body of a creature that "resemble(d) the Montauk Monster in a lot of ways," as he reported to the *Riverhead News-Review* in a March 30, 2011 feature by Tim Gannon entitled "Has a Montauk Monster washed ashore in Northville?"

The teenager, a Riverhead High School student named Jason Brown, e-mailed the newspaper some pictures he had taken while walking down Iron Pier Beach. According to the article, "A News-Review reporter walked the entire length of the beach on both sides of the boat ramp Wednesday, but, alas, no monster."

Kimberly Durham of the Riverhead Foundation for Marine Research and Preservation speculated that it was a raccoon carcass. As with the original Montauk Monster, the carcass disappeared, and all we have left is a photo and a story.

Yet another unidentified beast washed ashore dead under the Brooklyn Bridge in New York City on July 22, 2012. This one was photographed by Denise Ginley and was again compared to the Montauk Monster in its appearance. The New York City Parks Department opined that it was "a discarded cooked pig," but Ginley insisted "the feet are not pig-like at all . . . No hooves or cloven feet to be seen—it definitely had five toes on all its paws, front and back."

An article in the *New York Daily News* by Philip Caulfield published on July 25 noted that Ginley had discovered the carcass while strolling with her boyfriend along the Manhattan side of the East River. She took several photos, which all show a bizarre beast that blogger Joe Coscarelli noted looked like something "in between a rodent of unusual size and a part-human werewolf."

Dr. Paul Curtis, a Cornell University professor and wildlife specialist, felt that it "could be a small dog that ballooned with decay." The article concluded: "The waterlogged ghoul drew comparisons to the 'Montauk Monster,' which captivated New Yorkers after washing ashore on Ditch Plains beach in July 2008."

How many more strange beasts will wash ashore on the beaches of New York before someone identifies them? And why do the carcasses always vanish? Someone is obviously taking them, but for what purpose? Where the Montauk Monster and other bizarre beasts of New York are concerned, there are plenty of questions, but no answers.

Alien Creatures and Little People in the Hudson Valley

Everyone knows the story of Rip Van Winkle, the American colonist who, in the Catskill Mountains, is challenged to a game of nine-pins by the diminutive "ghosts" of Hendrick Hudson and his crew. Rip drinks some of their liquor and falls asleep, not awakening for twenty years, after the American Revolution has taken place. Washington Irving's whimsical tale was actually based on ancient stories of "fairy abduction," in which the Little People take mortals into the Land of Faerie where time has no meaning.

Irving may have based his story on a folktale from the Orkney Islands off Scotland, where there is a burial mound adjacent to the Ring of Brodgar, a Neolithic stone circle. In that story, a drunken fiddler on his way home hears ethereal music emanating from the mound, finds a way in, and discovers trolls having a wild party. He stays there and plays for two hours, then makes his way home, where he finds that fifty years have passed. Irving's father was from the Orkneys, and so he may very well have heard the tale when he was a child.

Native Americans, however, had remarkably similar legends, causing one to speculate that perhaps there is more truth to the legends of "Little People" than may be generally believed. The Cree, for example, an Algonquin-speaking people, believed in a race of tricksters they called the Mannegishi—small, semi-humanoids with thin arms, lanky legs, and large, noseless heads. Said to live between rocks in the river's rapids, the Mannegishi were thought to have delighted in crawling out of the rocks to capsize canoes, dragging boaters to watery deaths.

Algonquin tradition also spoke of the Memegwesi, hairy-faced dwarfs that dwelled on riverbanks. Often traveling in groups, they supposedly appeared only to those of "pure minds," which generally meant children. The similarities to the Celtic legends of fairies are startling. From where could such stories originate?

The Ojibwe, Algonquin, Abenaki, Wampanoag, and Mohican tribes also told tales of the pukwudgie, magical little people of the forest, again very similar to European legends of gnomes, fairies, and leprechauns. Stories of the pukwudgie were told throughout the northeastern United States as well as Canada and the Great Lakes region. Pukwudgies could be dangerous, but only to people who disrespected them. They were capricious beings who played harmless pranks, but at a whim might kidnap children or play vicious tricks that could turn deadly. Usually described as being about knee-high or smaller, the name pukwudgie literally meant "person of the wilderness," and they were said to have been spirits of the forest. In some traditions—again, echoing the Old World fairy stories—they had a sweet aroma and were associated with flowers. Their magical powers included the ability to become invisible, to confuse people's minds, or to transform into cougars or other ferocious animals. In another strong echo of European beliefs—the custom of the "Evil Eye"—they could cause harm to people merely by staring at them.

What is it about human beings around the world that makes them believe in a race of mischievous "Little People" who play tricks on people and sometimes cause them injury? There are even such tales in the Far East, particularly Japan. If a legend is so universally believed, could it have a basis in fact?

The key to this mystery may lie in the more recent stories of so-called alien abductions. The similarities are remarkable: the motif of "missing time" is present in both alien and fairy abductions. As we have seen, when fairies abduct mortals, they cause their abductees to enter some other dimension, a place where there is some type of paranormal lapse of time. Rip Van Winkle thought he had only been asleep for a few moments, but in fact he had been sleeping for twenty years in the Realm of Faerie.

There are also similarities in appearance between fairies and aliens. Fairies, of course, are small creatures, often with large, staring eyes. Some reports of alien abduction include descriptions of the diminutive beings holding "power rods" used to paralyze abductees, just as fairies were said to carry magic wands.

Another fascinating parallel between aliens and fairies is their predilection for stealing human babies. Abducting babies from cribs was a commonly described fairy activity, and sometimes the abductors replaced them with a "changeling," a fairy child left in the baby's place. Similarly, modern UFO lore includes accounts told by women of their abductions by aliens, during which they are impregnated; later, the women are kidnapped again, and the extraterrestrials remove the alien fetus from their wombs.

Fairies often dwelled in "mounds" in the woods; UFOs, which could be considered to be "mound-shaped," are allegedly often seen sitting on the ground in the woods at night. Indeed, author Whitley Strieber's abductions began in and around his isolated cabin in the Catskill Mountains—the same area where Rip Van Winkle was "abducted" by Hendrick Hudson and his men—in 1985.

Over the Christmas holidays, Strieber was staying with his wife and son in the cabin when his security alarm went off. He awakened to see a small, thin being with huge black eyes in his bedroom. The next thing he knew, he was sitting in the woods outside his cabin, his memories confused and fragmented. Eventually, to understand what had happened to him that night, he underwent regressive hypnosis with Dr. Donald F. Klein, which uncovered many of the details of his experience.

Under hypnosis, Strieber recalled that he had been "floated" out of his bedroom into a UFO that sat waiting in the woods. He saw four different types of alien beings: small, robot-like creatures; a short, thickly built type; slender, fragile-looking creatures; and a being with black, button-like eyes. This experience led Strieber to write his controversial book *Communion: A True Story*, which was published a couple years later. Since that time, Strieber has claimed to have undergone many more abductions and, contrary to popular belief, he has never claimed that the beings who abducted him were "aliens" from outer space. He refers to them only as "the visitors," and says that he has no idea where they come from.

Interestingly enough, the so-called "UFO Capital of New York" is not far from Strieber's former cabin (he doesn't stay there anymore—and who can blame him?). Pine Bush is a small town in northern Orange County, on the surface a typical suburban area. In his book *Weird New York*, Chris Gethard points out: "The Hudson Valley of New York has long been home to some truly weird occurrences. . . . most famously, the Hudson Valley has long been known to attract strange vessels and beings from outer space. Pine Bush has come to be known worldwide as the primary destination for these extra-terrestrial visitors in the area."

Although some residents of Pine Bush have shared their personal experiences of alien sightings and abductions dating back to the 1960s, the town's reputation as the UFO capital of New York—if not the entire East Coast—stems from a series of high-profile sightings that occurred between the mid-1980s on up into the 1990s. In the eighties there was a series of sightings of a mysterious craft called "The Westchester Wing" or "The Hudson Valley Boomerang." The flap involved thousands of eyewitnesses.

The UFO was an immense triangular or V-shaped object that was seen in the Hudson River area—mainly in Westchester County—just north of New York City. Between 1982 and 1995, more than seven thousand sightings were documented by a team of scientific researchers led by Philip J. Imbrogno, a high school science teacher and astronomer. The silent object often flew fairly close to the ground over the Taconic Parkway, so low that witnesses could observe its multicolored lights, which were linked by a gray structure. Hundreds of sightings were reported from neighboring Connecticut.

Bob Pratt, author of the book *Night Siege* with Imbrogno and famed UFO researcher J. Allen Hynek, noted: "It was enormous, awesome and spectacular. It moved slowly and silently and was easily as big as a football field; some witnesses said as big as three football fields. That would make it anywhere from 300 to 900 feet long, far larger than any aircraft manufactured in the world."

Witnesses came from all walks of life, but there were many professionals, including aircraft designers, nurses, doctors, pilots, engineers, and technicians of all stripes. Some skeptical police officers became much more open-minded when they saw the craft themselves.

During this unusually long UFO flap, many witnesses reported having had some kind of contact with alien beings; more than sixty people claimed to have been abducted by strange creatures, with young women between the ages of twenty-five and thirty—typical child-bearing age—representing an inordinate number of abduction cases. Sightings tapered off after 1986, but they have continued sporadically to this day. The FAA has consistently denied that anything odd was happening over the Hudson Valley, although some air traffic controllers privately admitted they had tracked unknown objects on radar.

While these sensational sightings were attracting a great deal of media attention, events that were just as strange—if not stranger—were quietly being reported with alarming frequency in Pine Bush. As Gethard pointed out in his book, "As the hype over the Westchester sightings died down, more and more people began to realize that truly strange, phenomenal things were occurring in the seemingly normal rural village."

Numerous residents of Pine Bush began reporting that they had seen a variety of unidentified aircraft, not just the boomerang-shaped object(s), but "pencil-thin" hovering craft, balls of light, and other types of craft. There were rumors of "strange strobe lights" that were seen in the woods outside the town, as well as reports of strange noises and sightings at the Jewish Cemetery on Route 52.

In 1991, Ellen Crystall released her book *Silent Invasion: The Shocking Discoveries of a UFO Researcher*. Crystall was a resident of New Jersey who had been visiting Pine Bush for eleven years and documenting UFO-related encounters from the locals. Her book included controversial photos of alien craft. The media started to pick up on what was happening in Pine Bush as a result of Crystall's book, and journalists began to conduct their own investigations there.

When Pine Bush residents began sharing their UFO stories with each other, they came to realize just how many there were. Some told of groups of dozens of UFOs flying over the town, and by the middle of the 1990s, the town became recognized as the UFO capital of the East Coast.

Large crowds of people began to gather nightly around the town, and they came to be known as "skywatchers" or "UFO-ers." The most-frequented area was at West Searesville Road, where hundreds of people reported seeing strange objects in the sky. The crowds became so large that the police were forced to ban the skywatchers, as they were disrupting traffic on the road.

Grass-roots movements, however, cannot be stopped so easily, and smaller groups still formed at South Searesville and at the Jewish Cemetery, where "unidentified animal sightings" allegedly occurred. Various local newspapers picked up on the stories: the *Times-Herald Record* reported a sighting by Pine Bush resident John Lewis, who videotaped a "thin black object" in the sky. Per the article: "Lewis watched the object move slowly downward at a forty-five degree angle for about five minutes . . . Then he rushed for his video camera. The unidentified flying object was pencil-shaped and black with a long tail. There was not a glint of reflection from the sun."

Another local, Bill Wiand, told the *Poughkeepsie Journal* about his encounter with aliens: "I did recently have an invasion and it terrified me . . . It started like it always does, with the noise in my ears and it just kind of rumbles through. I couldn't move my body, but I could move my eyes and I knew the room was filled with entities." The article also noted that there had been other local abductions, including one anonymous person who claimed, "They immobilized me and undressed me and put this device on my genitals and took a sperm sample."

Another report in the *Times-Herald* noted the claims of Pine Bush resident and sergeant at Woodbourne Correctional Facility Jim Smith, who reported: "I've seen so many of the beings, I know exactly how they move. They're different sizes, different shapes, but when you see them so much, you know they're not of this earth.

"Not long ago, I saw this figure about six foot six and dressed in all black standing beneath the traffic light in Pine Bush," Smith said. "When she moved, it wasn't like walking. It wasn't in frames either, like most of them move. In frames, they're someplace and then they're suddenly in another place, like time-lapse photography. But this one moved horizontally.

"In Pine Bush, you see things you don't expect. I've seen a cat with no head walking across the floor. It just had a piece of cardboard where the head should be. A lot of people in Pine Bush tell me they've seen that cat. But not everyone can see the cat or the beings. You have to be open to things like that."

Over the past twenty years, Pine Bush has seen a lot of construction and development and the UFO stories have died down somewhat. But the sightings of mysterious creatures and instances of "high strangeness," including what Gethard refers to as "shadowy figures, strange noises permeating desolate areas, flashing lights and more," are still being reported with some frequency. What is it about this little village that attracts such otherworldly beings? What, indeed, is it about the Hudson Valley?

I'd like to end this chapter with a few personal anecdotes.

If the Hudson Valley is in fact a haunted place, I grew up in one of its most haunted spots. I have already told you of my family's encounters with the so-called "Kinderhook Creature." What I have not told you is that it was not the only strange being that "haunted" the woods behind my grandparents' house.

When I was nine or ten years old, my cousin Chari and I were playing in the woods behind the house. We were near the top of the highest hill on the property, which adjoined a neighbor's land. It was late in the day, just before sundown, when we heard a high-pitched whistling sound from somewhere nearby. I turned and looked in the direction of where I thought the sound had come from, and, much to my shock, there was a white object seemingly peering at me from behind a huge old pine tree. I shouldn't really say it was "peering," as it had no eyes that I could see, but I had the feeling that it was looking at me. It looked like a huge, amorphous blob, and it scared me to death.

The closest I can get to a description of the thing is that it looked something like Casper the Friendly Ghost of animated cartoon fame: it had a big round "head" and there was a bluish tint to it. My cousin didn't really take the time to look; I told her we should get out of the woods and we both ran down the hill at great speed. We never looked back.

The thing that strikes me as really odd about this encounter—aside from the obvious—is the whistling sound that attracted our attention in the first place. If this had been the only encounter with such a bizarre creature in our woods, I may have passed it off as childish imagination. It was not, however.

Two or three years later, on a sunny August afternoon just before my twelfth birthday, my friend Jerome Miller had been walking through the woods alone when he came running up to the house. Looking as pale as a ghost himself, he told me upon catching his breath that he had just seen a "big white blob" gliding down the hill towards him. The sight of it had frightened him so much that he had jumped clear over a six-foot-wide pond during his mad dash to the house.

At first I thought he was pulling my leg, but then I realized that I had never told him about my encounter with a similar entity a few years before. I told him we should go back into the woods and attempt to track the thing down.

And so the two of us, pitchforks in hand—what good we thought they would do I'll never know—tramped into the woods to find the thing. And we did. We saw it, and perhaps it saw us, whatever "it" was. Jerome stopped suddenly on the trail and pointed straight ahead without saying a word. I looked in the direction he was pointing and saw a large white shape that seemed to hover in the trees. Our childhood bravado left us immediately: I shouted, "My gosh, let's get out of here!" and we dropped our pitchforks and ran for the house.

The story gets stranger and stranger, because sightings of the "blob" spanned generations. I never told my cousins Barry Knights or Russell Zbierski about my sightings of the "blob" either, but that didn't prevent them from seeing the same thing, or something similar, more than sixteen years later. The two of them had been at a lean-to they had constructed in the woods, near the same area where Jerome and I had our encounters when we were kids. Barry told me they had seen a "white, almost bell-shaped kind of thing" that had glided or floated down the hill toward them.

The story of the "blob" does not end there, however. Another fifteen years later, my father was out on his tractor doing some work on his property when something "big and white" flew over his head. He only saw it for an instant before it vanished into the woods, but he described it as looking like a "shmoo," a cartoon creature created by Al Capp in the classic comic strip "L'il Abner" in 1948. A shmoo was supposedly a white, amorphous creature that lived in the forest. My father had used his own frame of reference to describe what was essentially the same thing that had been seen by my friend Jerome, my cousins, and myself.

There have been other strange occurrences near my grandparents' home. One fine evening in 1974, my grandmother and I gazed in wonder upon a light show in the sky that we could see from our picture window in the dining room, which looked out over the Catskill Mountains. In the sky were several orange balls of light that were flying about as the sun was setting. At first, they were separate—four or five of them—and they were doing seemingly impossible maneuvers, such as 360-degree turns and then stopping dead in the sky, then circling around again, then all getting together in a cluster, then separating again. We watched these objects—which we were convinced were intelligently controlled—for about ten minutes, before they all flew off in complete silence into various points in the sky and disappeared.

This may have happened in the same year that my grandmother and I saw the little man in green digging for something on our property. I was out walking in the field one day when I saw this fellow digging at the edge of the woods on our land. It was pretty unusual to see strangers on our property, and a little unnerving in this case, because the man was dressed entirely in green—green shirt, green pants, green hat—and he was shoveling away as if looking for something important in the soil. I called out to him and he ignored me, shoveling like mad as if digging for buried treasure.

I decided to go and get my grandmother, and she came out to the field with me. We both called out to the man, and at one point he turned to look at us. The eerie thing was that, despite the fact it was a beautiful, sunny afternoon and he was only a few yards from us, we couldn't see any features on his face. Then he simply turned around again and went back to his digging.

The whole encounter had been so unsettling that we decided, as witnesses to strange occurrences often do, to shut it out: we simply walked back to the house and went inside. Decades later, I still don't know why we did that. At some point a few minutes later, we thought perhaps we should go out again and see if the man was still there. We went back to the field and he was gone. In fact, not only was there no man there, there was no sign of anyone having dug up the soil at the edge of the woods.

This encounter was one of the strangest things that has ever happened to me. I've often wondered who—or what—we saw that day. A man dressed in green, digging as if for buried treasure?

All of which brings us back to where we began this chapter, with stories of little people, both ancient and modern, in the Hudson Valley. Be they fairies or aliens or what Whitley Strieber calls "the visitors," something bizarre seems to dwell in this region, of which Washington Irving wrote: "A drowsy, dreamy influence seems to hang over the land, and to pervade the very atmosphere."

Catamounts and Other Mystery Beasts

The New York State Department of Environmental Conservation (DEC) website says the following in regards to the Eastern cougar:

> The Eastern cougar, or mountain lion, is listed as an endangered species in New York. This animal was historically present in the state, but has been absent since the late 1800s . . . Officially cougars are considered extirpated from the state; however, sightings of animals believed to be cougars are commonly reported to DEC wildlife offices.
>
> To date, no hard evidence has been produced that would prove the existence of cougars living and reproducing in the wild in New York . . . Wildlife staff will only investigate reports where physical evidence is likely or known to exist, or when a captive animal has been reported to have escaped.

As this official statement indicates, reports of cougars, mountain lions, and catamounts continue to pour in. The DEC was forced to eat a little bit of crow in 2011, when an article by Don Lehman, titled "DEC Confirms Wild Mountain Lion in Lake George," appeared in the August 19 edition of the *Glens Falls Post-Star*:

"State wildlife biologists have confirmed that a wild mountain lion passed through Warren County last winter before it was hit and killed by a car in Connecticut earlier this year.

'A series of DNA analyses have linked it to mountain lion fur left behind with cat paw prints in the back yard of a Lake George home last December,' said Lori Severino, a spokeswoman for the State Department of Environmental Conservation."

The article went on to state that, although the big cat was believed to have been native to South Dakota, it was the first "confirmed" cougar presence in the region since a small mountain lion was killed in Saratoga County in 1993. That animal was found to have been native to South America and was believed to have escaped from captivity.

DEC wildlife biologist Kevin Hynes noted, "This sighting turns out to be part of a remarkable and fascinating case . . . It is interesting to note that this one lone mountain lion passing through New York was detected and confirmed through track photographs and DNA . . . which is good evidence that if a population of mountain lions lived in the northeastern U.S., they would likely be detected."

Earlier in 2011, the U.S. Fish and Wildlife Service had declared the Eastern cougar to be extinct. No matter where this particular 140-pound adult male specimen may have come from, the only thing that caused it to become "extinct" was that it had been hit by a car. Cougars in New York State are not phantoms; they are real, flesh and blood creatures that eat, reproduce, and die, whether or not the DEC accepts that fact.

As David Baron wrote in an opinion piece in the *New York Times*, "You have to appreciate this cat's sense of irony . . .

The cougar showed up in the East just three months after the Fish and Wildlife Service declared the eastern cougar extinct, a move that would exempt the officially nonexistent sub-species of the big cat from federal protection. Perhaps this red-state cougar traveled east to send a message to Washington: the federal government can make pronouncements about where cougars are not supposed to be found, but a cat's going to go where a cat wants to go."

People had been reporting "big cats" in New York State for many years prior to the 2011 road kill. On December 2, 2005, the Oneonta, New York *Daily Star* reported that two local men saw what appeared to be a mountain lion or cougar cross the road in front of them as they drove up to the woods to hunt deer. In response to this story, John Lutz, co-founder of the Eastern Puma Research Network, contradicted the DEC's stance on the issue: "I'd like to set the record straight . . . There are definitely WILD big cats in the Empire State. The majority of WILD mountain lions are in the Adirondack Park Region, but smaller populations survive in the Catskills and Finger Lakes Regions."

Joe Biello relayed his own report to the website Crypto-mundo in 2005:

I have seen something of the sort in lower New York State, just thirty-five miles north of Manhattan! I live in Rockland County, New York, and back in the early nineties there was a flurry of big cat sightings by my house. People who lived on the mountain saw it in their yards and described it as a small mountain lion! I was driving home one night and just beyond the reach of my headlights on a road that is right beside this moun-tain was a large low creeping animal with a long flat tail and it was a dusky tan color. It got across the road before my light completely hit it and was into the woods . . . In Harriman state park which is another twenty miles north of me there was a family that lived at one of the camps year round and she had multiple sightings of a cougar while she lived there.

Another Cryptomundo reader known only as "Desimone" reported: "My brother was driving on Route 351 in Poestenkill, New York (Rensselaer County) . . . when he saw a mountain lion on the side of the road. He drove by very slowly and it crouched down. There was no doubt that it could be any other animal; my brother knows what a mountain lion looks like and he drove by it at about five miles per hour so he got a good long look at it. His boss who lives in Ravena, New York (Albany County) has a small farm with a few cows and he says he saw a mountain lion on his land on two different occasions in 2006. They are definitely in New York!"

On September 11, 2012, the *New York Post* featured a story about a "big cat on the loose near New York's swanky holiday destination, The Hamptons." The reports described "a grayish cat-like creature about five feet long, two feet high at the shoulder with a long striped tail," according to DEC spokesman Bill Fonda. The cat sprinted into the brush before officials could spot it, but some were calling it "a jaguar." Needless to say, Fonda opined, "There's not sufficient evidence of a cougar, panther, jaguar or similar exotic creature."

While this particular beast could have been an escaped pet, other sightings cannot be so easily explained. Stewart Lindsay, a Yahoo! contributor, wrote a 2010 piece for that web search engine entitled "Big Cats in Western New York," which made some interesting points:

Rumors are flying in western New York about the sight-ing(s) of Mountain Lions; a species supposedly not found in New York state since approximately 1880 . . . These same spokespeople will tell us that there are no

Lynx in New York either. Even though New York shares an international boundary with the country that gave us the Canadian Lynx, these experts of all wild things claim that anyone who thinks they have spotted a Lynx has most likely just seen a bobcat or even just a very large house cat.

Lindsay went on to note that there were other creatures that weren't supposed to exist in New York, but which have proven their presence there over the years:

> There were no coyotes in western New York. All you had to do was check with any DEC office and they would tell you that if you saw one, you had probably just seen a small German Shepherd or some other breed of dog . . . they are now a very common wild visitor to many yards and fields in the region . . . Coyotes have probably been residents of western New York for much longer than the DEC wants to admit.

It is more or less accepted, then—except perhaps by the DEC—that cougars or catamounts still exist in New York State. Now that we've passed that hurdle, we must go on to the next one: what do we make of sightings of so-called "black panthers" in the state?

According to an April 2, 2009, post entitled "Big Black Cat Sightings: NY Black Cat Mystery," by Maggie M. Thorton on www.rightpundits.com, "Big Black Cat sightings in New York are escalating. Those who have seen the animal say it is definitely not a large house cat. . . reports of Big Black Cats crossing highways . . . in the State's Tallman National Park, and of most concern, in neighborhood backyards where children may be, keep rolling in."

According to the post, the cats are described as being four to five feet in length with tails approximately three feet long.

Thorton continued: "We might think a pranking is in the works, but in New York's Rockland County Park, the reports are taken seriously. Signs are posted warning the public of 'suspicious animal sightings.' In the hamlet of Palisades, one Big Black Cat was seen in a private drive and two in the backyard of the home. In Orangetown, police increased patrols and cameras have been installed in state parks."

Thorton went on to note that Great Britain has a long history of what she refers to (always capitalized) as "Big Black Cat" sightings. They're usually referred to as pumas or panthers. Thorton concluded her piece by saying, "Whatever the genus of the Big Black Cats in New York State, these animals are frightening people."

Dorian Tunnel was a witness to the "panther" sighting in Tallman State Park on March 17, 2009. According to Kirk Leavitt on the Yahoo! Contributor Network, "[Tunnel] was bike riding with his son when he heard a thrashing sound in the woods. He then saw a large black panther jumping over a rock about twenty-five yards away. He spotted a second big cat crouched as if waiting in ambush." The story stated that Tunnel noted that both cats had "a very shiny black coat of fur." He and his son were able to avoid the beasts without incident.

The story continued: "Grace Knowlton of Palisades, New York had heard the stories of the black panther sighting but did not give them much thought. Then on March 14, 2009, she spotted a large black panther crossing her lawn. She states that it was much larger than any domestic cat. She describes the animal as being pitch black with a shiny coat."

A note here about so-called "black panthers": this is not actually a species of feline, but rather a phrase used to describe a wild cat with black fur, such as a leopard or jaguar. Leopards are native to Africa and Asia, while jaguars were once found in the southwestern areas of the U.S., but were hunted to extinction by farmers whose livelihood was threatened by the beasts preying on their livestock in the late nineteenth century.

As Loren Coleman pointed out in his book *Mysterious America*, when people speak of black panthers, they are usually referring to leopards: "Within any litter of spotted leopards, the chances are high that one of the kits will be black. Among leopards of Asia, especially, the frequency of births and survival of black offspring is common . . . Some laymen have wrongly viewed the black leopard as a separate species and labeled them 'black panthers.' Since most people sense that a majority of the mystery cats are reported to be black, the phantom felines are thus tagged 'black panthers' by the press and the witnesses."

In his August 20, 2009, Yahoo! post, Leavitt wrote, "Professional tracker Shane Hobel believes that he has found proof of these black panthers in the Palisades, New York area. He has found the tracks of what he believes to be a big cat. The tracks were found in an area where he has found more and more deer kills that are different from the normal coyote kills. Hobel has also located what he believes to be the claw marks of a large cat on a tree in the area."

Scott Lope, director of the organization Big Cat Rescue, believes that some of the New York sightings may be a result of misidentification; it is, after all, difficult to judge the size of an animal from a distance, especially at night or at dusk or dawn. It is possible that the eyewitnesses may be seeing "a black lab or a large domestic cat," according to Lope.

There may be another explanation, however. Lope believes that it is possible that some witnesses may have seen "an escaped exotic animal." There are more than fifteen thousand big cats in captivity in the U.S., only a few of them in actual zoos. Some states don't regulate their ownership; while New York City alone is home to 103 registered "big cats," there may be hundreds more that are unregistered.

In his Yahoo! post, Leavitt went on to write: "The first captive big cat brought to the United States was a leopard that was displayed in New York in 1768. Since that time, the number of captive big cats has grown along with the number of escapes and attacks."

Leavitt's piece was titled "The MonsterQuest Search for Black Panthers in New York," and detailed the efforts of the History Channel television series *MonsterQuest* to find proof of the existence of big cats in New York in an episode called "Tigers in the Suburbs." The program sent four experts to Palisades to investigate the black panther sightings. Animal tracker Mark Peterson, photographer Jeremy Holden, and wildlife expert Dick Pearson headed the search for the black panther, while mammal expert Dr. Esteban Sarmiento was brought in to examine their evidence.

Peterson, Holden, and Pearson placed motion-sensing wireless cameras throughout the woods and installed infrared cameras. On their first night, they set up a blind near some game trails and used decoy calls to attract animals. They had no cat sightings, however.

Meanwhile, Sarmiento met with tracker Shane Hobel to take a look at the tracks and claw marks he had found. Sarmiento felt that the tracks were too small to be those of a tiger or lion and that perhaps they might belong to a leopard, which would make sense; as we have seen, leopards can indeed be black.

After reviewing all the evidence, the group felt that an escaped exotic cat may have been what people were reporting, with a leopard as the most likely suspect. Leavitt concluded his piece by stating, "While no definitive proof of a black panther could be found in New York, many experts agree that it is possible for this creature to exist. The most likely explanation would be an escaped big cat from a private owner."

All of this begs the question: if a big cat escaped from its owner, why wouldn't the owner report it? The answer: liability. As Lope explained, "These animals start out as cute cubs and quickly grow into fearsome predators that their owners may not know what to do with. If one escapes, the owner may not report this to authorities out of fear of liability."

Loren Coleman, however, thinks the answer to the big cat mysteries is more complex. In *Mysterious America*, he theorizes: "A good phantom panther report cannot be shrugged off so easily. The conventionalists, unwilling to admit they are stumped, usually try to ignore the mystery cats, or try to explain them away in terms of known animals . . . In the Northeast, in northern Maine, in the Appalachians of New York State, and in the Great Smokies of the Southeast . . . the eastern puma appears to be making a comeback."

Coleman went on to write that these "phantom panther" reports have elements of the paranormal: "Witnesses have shot at them without apparent effect, wildlife officials have set traps, sheriffs have conducted 'safaris,' and many people have done everything possible to bring a specimen in for examination. The mystery cats possess that weird tangible intangibility that makes understanding so difficult and investigation so frustrating."

A New York State conservationist once called these mystery cats "feline flying saucers." The more one investigates reports of all types of cryptids in New York State, in fact, the farther one travels down the rabbit hole in the direction of Wonderland.

For example, there was the bizarre beast sighted by several people in Queensbury during the summer of 2010. Steve Kulls wrote in the *Glens Falls Post Star* of August 1: "According to witnesses, the animal was light colored and appeared hairless, though perhaps with very short gray or blonde hair. It had pale blue round eyes, a long tail, kind of catlike, and stood like a dog but had a swagger like a cat. The snout was shaped like that of a kangaroo, not big like a dog and not flat like a cat. Its ears were flat against its head, not pointy or upright like a fox's, yet not floppy like a retriever's."

The description of the animal was similar to that of a so-called "chupacabra," a blood-sucking mystery beast whose name literally means "goat-sucker" in Spanish. The chupacabra has allegedly been sighted in Texas and throughout Mexico and Central America.

What could such a creature, if indeed it exists, be doing in New York State?

An anonymous blogger posted a curious report on a Westchester County website on July 8, 2012, that read, in part: "My husband and I saw an animal in our back yard this evening, and we're not sure what it was. It looked almost like a mix of fox/coyote/domestic dog . . . Very long tail. Not super thick like a coyote, but covered in fur . . . Head/ears looked like a cross between coyote and fox . . . Anyone out there seen anything like this in Northern Westchester County?"

One reply posted was: "Maybe it's a chupacabra."

Then there was the strange creature with a long neck that was seen in the Finger Lakes region, as reported by "Paige" on the Yahoo! Questions website during the summer of 2012: "My mother and I were driving through the Finger Lakes area today around dusk. We both saw a figure, maybe a foot high, with a long neck. I thought it had two legs, but my mother claims it had four. It almost resembled a small emu or kind of like a pterodactyl.

"It walked/ran across the road as we slowed down. Once it went into the weeds on the side of the road, it hopped straight up, I'd say about four feet up.

"We drove away quickly, and both of us were positive we saw it. It was not a cat, coyote, dog or crow or anything you might suggest. We have been in the area before and asked locals right after. I tried googling it. Nothing seems to explain it."

What can one make of such reports? With the return of the catamount to New York State, can other mystery beasts be taken as seriously? It's perhaps best to remember what Ivan T. Sanderson wrote: "We'll never catch them." And perhaps that's for the best. After all, then there would be no more mystery.

Appendix 1

CHAMP SIGHTINGS IN NEW YORK

1819
Bulwagga Bay: Captain Crum saw an animal he described as 187 feet long with a body the width of a hog's head. Its head, held more than fifteen feet above the water, was flat and had a mouth with three teeth—two in the center and one in the upper jaw. The head was black with white on its forehead. There was a belt of red around the neck.

1865
Whitehall: A Mr. Parker spotted a "large snake eighteen to twenty feet long" take to the water.

Mid-1860s
South Bay: Mark Doherty and two other people saw an immense snake while fishing from their boat. The sea serpent was trailing a five-pound catfish that the group had hooked.

1871
Barber Point: The passengers of the steamship *Curlew* saw an animal "traveling at railroad speed."

1873

Dresden: A group of people observed a beast at a range of one hundred feet traveling at a great speed. There was another sighting in Dresden that year by John French and his family, who said that the monster resembled a large tree with a raised head, and that it was moving with great force and speed into a strong wind.

1875

Dresden: C. N. Wood and Rev. J. W. Sands saw a creature they described as "log-like" and which they believed to be a "monster."

1879

Near the Bouquet River: Frederick Fairchild observed a beast that he said "resembled a large Newfoundland dog."

1882

Willsboro Bay: George Wilkins and his wife observed the creature in the bay.

1883

Cumberland Bay: Capt. Nathan H. Mooney, the Clinton County sheriff, had a sighting while on board the boat *Nellie.* He described the creature as twenty-five feet long and seven inches in diameter, with its head at least four or five feet out of the water. The neck was curved and the head was triangular and flat, with a nose shaped like a V.

1886

Cumberland Bay: Three men saw a beast about fifteen feet long with a head about fifteen to eighteen inches in length. The head was raised two feet above the water.

Essex: An unidentified man on the railroad tracks above the lake observed a "snake" that was twenty feet long with an eel-type head as large as a man's. The tail was also shaped like that of an eel.

Willsboro Point: S. W. Clark and others saw a "dark body" through a spyglass. Also in Willsboro Point, D. Brown observed a creature "like a long log or pole" while he was out in a boat.

1887

Bulwagga Bay: Workers from the Port Henry Ore and Iron Company and the Lake Champlain and Moriah Railroad Company claimed they saw the "Lake Champlain Sea Serpent" while they were laying railroad tracks.

Split Rock: A fishing party observed the "sea serpent" while they were fishing near the Split Rock ore bed.

Willsboro Point: Winford Morhous, Hiram Morhous and his wife, and their hired girl observed the head of an animal rising out of the water, its speed faster than the average steamboat.

1894

Cumberland Head: In a rare sighting of the "monster" on land, Luther Hagar, Tim Miller, Frank Dominy, and Ephraim Allen said they saw the beast and described it as dark on top and lighter in appearance on the bottom. They claimed that it came six feet or more out of the water and onto the shore.

1915

Bulwagga Bay: Several local inhabitants observed something in the bay with their field glasses that was more than forty feet long.

1918

South Bay: Frank Burrough observed an animal with a ridge of fifteen long fins on its back. He claimed that the creature had a round head with jaws like an alligator and that its skin was smooth.

1937

Whitehall: Gene McCabe, Coots Gordon, and Pat Harvey saw a creature about fifty feet long with a flowing red mane, eyes the size of dinner plates, moose-like antlers, and "elephant ears" while they were fishing from a pier on the lake.

Chimney Point: Capt. Johnny Blair and a deckhand who were on the lake in an oil tanker observed an animal sixty feet long and eight feet tall, with sharp scales along its back, broad flippers, and "hard" skin.

1939

Rouses Point: A couple in a boat saw a large animal surface and loop around toward their vessel.

1940

Plattsburgh: Robert Hughes, a guard at the Plattsburgh Military Barracks, saw the head, neck, and hump of a large animal in the lake.

1943

Rouses Point: Charles Weston observed a "huge reptile" through his binoculars, and said that the animal "churned up" water.

1945

Rouses Point: Charles Langlois and his wife observed a creature they described as fifteen to twenty feet long and "thick as a keg." They claimed that they came close enough to it in their rowboat to "whack it with an oar."

Near Fort Ticonderoga: Passengers on the ferryboat U.S. *Ticonderoga* observed a large animal's head break the water while they were in the middle of the lake watching a bridge-opening ceremony.

1946

Rouses Point: Mrs. Henry G. Augins, H. G. Augins, Mr. and Mrs. Martin Davis, and Mr. and Mrs. Fred Chevalier saw an animal eighteen to twenty feet in length in the lake.

1951

Valcour Island: Theresa Megargee and her husband saw a creature approximately thirty feet long opposite the island. She saw it three times that year, while her husband saw it once with her. The third time she shot at it with a rifle, but apparently missed.

1961

North Bay: Thomas E. Morse, a student driver, observed a gray, thirty- to fifty-foot-long "eel-like" creature that crawled out of the water and onto the shore.

1964

West Bay: Joan Weissbecker, Jud Ellenwood, and others saw several humps in the water, as well as the head of the beast, which was described as "about the size of a grapefruit."

1966

Whallon Bay: Anne P. Marsh observed an animal that she estimated was between fifteen and eighteen feet long, with coils and a black, snake-like head.

1967

Bulwagga Bay: While fishing from a boat, Gordon F. Baker saw a "greenish-gray" animal more than twenty feet long swimming in the lake.

1970

Essex: Previous witness Anne P. Marsh and several others on the deck of a ferry saw a black-colored creature between fifteen to eighteen feet long swimming slowly through the water. She observed it with binoculars.

Cumberland Head: William Bianchi and Edward E. Taylor saw one or possibly two creatures. Two portions, each between ten and fifteen feet long and twelve to eighteen inches in diameter, were sighted. Each was shiny black.

1971

Port Henry: In February, some townspeople saw a creature break through the ice near the Velez Marina and then descend back under the ice.

Valcour Island: While driving on Route 9, Vincent and Dawn Iamunno observed a "monster" estimated at between fifty to seventy feet long, fifteen feet in width, and six to ten feet in height. It was grayish in color.

Bulwagga Bay: Dick Sherman and John Genier were working at a restaurant overlooking the bay when they saw "several humps" in the lake at a distance of three hundred and four hundred yards.

Bulwagga Bay: Richard E. Gilbo and Walter E. Wojewodzic were putting up a duck blind when they observed three grayish humps measuring more than forty feet long and three feet high from about one hundred yards away.

1973

Essex: While boating, John F. Durant and his father saw three gray humps.

North West Bay: Gretna Longware and several other people were at a marina when they saw something described as having a "gray dorsal fin" in the lake.

Port Henry: Louis Velez, Mike Atner, and others observed a hump or wake between eighteen to twenty feet long that was dark or black in color. They boarded a boat with an outboard motor and chased the creature until it descended into Crab Harbor.

Keeseville: From a canoe, Christina and Philip Putnam observed an animal measuring between sixteen to eighteen feet in length with "its head raised like a periscope."

Essex: From a ferry crossing the lake, Edward A. Manship Jr. observed a forty- to sixty-foot long animal that was raised "up to one foot" out of the water.

1974

Cumberland Head: Lynn Webster and Ted Wild saw a creature in the lake, describing the creature's head as "something that resembled a stove pipe."

1975

Port Henry: While driving north along the lakeshore, Lenus Drinkwine and his wife saw an animal that was approximately thirty feet long and "three feet in height out of the water" swimming in the lake.

Port Henry: From a hovercraft, C. W. Putnam observed an animal that he compared to a "Florida manatee" in appearance, gray with scale-less skin. The creature rose about four feet out of the water.

Port Henry: Restaurant owner Robert Blye and his patrons observed a creature between twenty to thirty feet long and with two dark-colored humps.

Plattsburgh: From the rear deck of a ferry, Mrs. John Grigas and three other people saw something with "a dog's head and two humps" swimming in the lake.

North West Bay: From a house overlooking the bay, Janet Tyler saw a black creature in the lake that was estimated at seven feet long and a foot wide.

1976

Corlear Bay: Nancy Warren and her family saw a creature, dark or black in color, with its head and neck three feet above the water, frolicking in the lake.

Treadwell Bay: Orville Wells saw something in the bay that was around twenty feet long, its head upright with a long neck and brownish in color.

Ausable River: Norm Foote and others saw a ten-foot-long animal near the mouth of the river that they thought "could be a sturgeon."

1977

Clinton Community College: Roger and Larry Lorberbaum observed a black twenty- to thirty-foot-long animal in the lake not far from the college.

1978

Cumberland Head: Nancy S. Robinson and her family saw something that "looked like the old Sinclair Dinosaur," a reference to the brontosaurus logo of the former Sinclair Oil Company. The creature was approximately twelve feet long, with its head sticking seven and a half feet out of the water.

Essex: Mr. and Mrs. James Newell and Carolyn Benn observed three sections of a creature, each of which around ten feet long, and which they described as "serpent-like" and gray or black.

Plattsburgh: Capt. Richard M. Dickson was fishing from a jetty near the Plattsburgh Air Force Marina when he observed three or four dark brown or black humps in the lake.

Bulwagga Bay: Marge and Melvin Grandjean saw a creature that was twelve feet long, with the dark-colored "bony back part of its head" jutting out of the water.

Essex: Colleen Van Hoven and her son observed ten to fifteen feet of "dark area" moving just below the surface of the lake.

Bulwagga Bay: From a restaurant overlooking the bay, Alice Mazuzan observed two black humps in the water.

1979

Valcour Island: Clark Winslow and several others aboard a boat saw something animate in the lake. They estimated that it was between twenty and twenty-five feet long and one and a half feet high.

Cumberland Head: Nancy S. Robinson and her family again saw something that "looked like the old Sinclair Dinosaur" holding its head high out of the water.

Port Henry: Alice Pratt saw an animal that was around twenty feet long and black swimming in the lake.

1980

Port Henry: Milo Drake saw a thirty-foot-long creature with three large humps and smooth, dark gray skin. The animal protruded two feet out of the water.

Cumberland Head: Nancy S. Robinson and her family claimed their third sighting of a beast that Robinson said "looked like the Sinclair Dinosaur."

Plattsburgh: Crystal Cadieux and Craig Mowry were driving along the lake when they observed a dark green head and neck about five to six feet out of the water.

1981

Fort Ticonderoga: Doug Morse Jr. and Tammy Burke saw approximately six feet of an animal's length out of the water, comprising two black humps.

Bulwagga Bay: Barbara Boyle, Carmilla K. Rich, Jane Sullivan, and Esther Waldron saw a thirty- to forty-foot-long creature (and possibly its head) that was black or dark brown.

Port Henry: Robert E. Hughes and his family saw an animal just under the surface of the lake. It was reportedly twenty-five to thirty feet long and black or dark green.

Westport: First from ashore and later from a boat, W. Jay Kohen and his family and friends observed a twenty-foot-long beast with a large hump and "jagged" back that was black.

Port Henry: Norma Manning, Ann Manning, and Michael Manning saw a ten-foot-long, dark brown animal in the lake.

Rock Harbor: George H. Bunnell and Mr. and Mrs. J. Marchelewicz were aboard a sloop when they observed about a five- to six-foot portion of an animal with ridges on its back. Its neck was seen and it was slimy and dark in color. They claimed that Champ moved up and down "like a dolphin or porpoise."

Bulwagga Bay: Kelly J. Williams and several other people observed something from shore that was black, over thirty feet long, and with its head partially out of the water. One of their photographs of the creature appeared in the August 1982 issue of *Life* magazine.

Port Henry: Gerald Williams Jr. saw a creature with its head raised four to five feet out of the water. Its eyes measured between six and seven inches in diameter. The animal was either shiny black or dark gray.

Bulwagga Bay: Gary Michener saw a dark, possibly black beast measuring between thirty and forty feet long, with twelve to fourteen humps. He said that the humps rose and fell as the creature moved.

Bulwagga Bay: From a twelve-foot boat, Claude Van Kleeck and several others observed a creature not less than fifty feet long and at least as wide as a fifty-five gallon barrel. The beast swam in an "up and down" fashion. Van Kleeck said that the animal was swimming at a speed of no less than forty miles per hour.

1982

Long Point: Raymond W. Sargent was boating when he saw about eighteen to twenty-four inches of a head and neck rise above the surface of the water. After the creature submerged, Sargent said that when his boat passed over the area of his sighting, his "sonar depth sounder became erratic, showing a blip at every digit on the scale markings."

Bulwagga Bay: Theresa Whitaker, Nina W. Mandy, and several others saw a twenty-foot-long, grayish-black animal with three humps.

Bulwagga Bay: Susan Sherman and Carol Anson saw an animal basking in the sun. The creature had an oval-shaped head and a long, snakelike neck and was dark green.

Bulwagga Bay: John and Nina W. Mandy observed three black humps that left a wake behind them.

Port Henry: Debbie Towne saw three humps of something that "looked like a giant snake" and was black or very dark green.

Bulwagga Bay: Claude Van Kleeck, Ed Avery, and Sam and Joyce Ruggles observed a blackish-gray animal that was between forty-five and fifty feet long and had a "serpent-shaped" head.

Rouses Point: John Annette and Michael Dumar saw something between twelve and twenty feet long that swam like an eel. Dumar said that the head "looked like a periscope sticking out of the water."

King Bay: Edward Sheldon, Shawn Elvidge, and Dan Ormsby saw a large black animal that looked like "a huge snake with three humps." They claimed that it brushed up against a sailboat while leaving the bay.

Rouses Point: About thirty people saw an animal with three humps that submerged after being buzzed by a seaplane.

Rouses Point: Cathy Cooper saw a black, three-humped animal in the lake.

1983

Crown Point: Barbara and Theresa Drinkwine and one other unnamed witness saw a large creature with its head sticking up out of the water.

Chazy Landing: Beverly Fraser saw a "dark shadow" that was between ten and fifteen feet long swimming underwater.

Cumberland Head: Robert and Kevin Alger were near a lighthouse when they observed something just under the water and a black fin breaking the water. Alger believed that he saw two creatures, one behind the other.

Plattsburgh: Joe and Toni Krupka saw a twenty- to thirty-foot long animal with three to four black ridges.

Crown Point: Ronald S. Kermani and Susan Kopp were fishing from a rowboat when they saw two humps in the water that were about two feet in height. They said that the humps were dark in color and undulated as they moved at speeds between one and two miles per hour.

Willsboro: Jane Marsh and Mrs. Kimball Prince claimed that they observed two twenty-foot long "monsters" through their binoculars.

Rouses Point: Mrs. Betty Hebert and her family said that they saw a ten-foot-long animal with two black humps swimming in the lake.

Port Henry: Kelly and Brande Pratt, along with several other people, saw bubbles in the lake before two humps appeared.

Bulwagga Bay: Hank Gilbo was in a boat when he heard a noise like "a gurgling sound." He then observed what looked like "a snout, brownish color, sticking about a foot out of the water." He took 8mm film footage of what he saw, but the results were inconclusive.

Crown Point: Claire Salaway heard "a strange sound" and saw "a long thing, larger than a boat."

Port Henry: Bess Sherlock and her husband were fishing when they saw a large, dark gray animal "like a snake."

Port Henry: From the beach, Michelle Baker and two other people saw a dark green or black, twenty-five- to thirty-five-foot-long animal swimming against the current. No head or neck was visible, but several humps were spotted. The creature appeared as small waves, and then rose above the surface and was viewed for ten or fifteen seconds before it gradually submerged again.

1986

Willsboro Point: Scott Gifford and his grandmother Ida Gifford were fishing when their attention was drawn to splashing in the lake. They observed something with "a series of large fins" about eighteen inches high protruding from the water. Then the creature, which Scott said "appeared to be thirty feet long," came within thirty yards of their boat.

Port Henry: Robert Pell-deChame was driving on Route 9N near Bulwagga Bay when he saw the "tail" of something very big in the lake. He pulled off to the side of the road and looked at the large ripples in the lake, while four to five other drivers did the same thing until the object submerged.

2005

Near Ausable River: Two fishermen in a boat, Peter Bodette and Dick Affolter, saw and videotaped a large animal that made a "strange wake" in the water. As Affolter noted of the video, "There is something in the water . . . just under the surface." Bodette told ABC News that the creature was "as big around as my thigh." The video appears to show, among other things, a dorsal fin.

2009

Plattsburgh: Carl Roberts and some friends were fishing off Wilcox Dock when they saw something large moving in the water about one hundred yards away. Roberts noted, "It had to be fifty feet long, from what I could see of the humps . . . It was so close that I could see the texture of its skin." He also noted that the creature's skin was "whale-like."

Appendix 2

BIGFOOT SIGHTINGS IN NEW YORK

1604

St. Lawrence River: French explorer Samuel de Champlain logs Micmac Indian stories concerning the "gouge," a giant, hairy humanoid.

1818

Sackets Harbor: A local man observes a "wild man" emerge from the woods and approach him before it turns and runs back into the forest.

1893

Rockaway: A large "wild man" with "bloodshot eyes and long, flowing, matted hair" is seen on the shore of the Rockaway inlet by "Red" McDowell and George Farrell, who are rowing a boat.

Rockaway: John Louth observed a large, hairy "wild man" near some trees in Rockaway Park.

Rockaway: Susie Louth was struck on her back by a "wild man" who had leapt from some brush; he knocked her to the ground and ran off.

Rockaway: Plumber William Tweedle was hunting when he was attacked by a "wild man" that was eating a raw chicken. The creature threw Tweedle to the ground and ran off.

Rockaway: House mover John Corning and his assistant William McVay were working near the beach when a "wild man" attacked them and ran away.

Rockaway: "Ned" Tracy shouted at a hairy "wild man" that was eating raw clams near the shore. The creature ran off.

Rockaway: Police Chief McArthur's wife was seized from behind and nearly choked by a "creature" that was chased away by friend Fred Sauer.

Margaretville: Farmer William Cook was attacked by a "wild man" said to be about seven feet tall and with "big teeth." Cook shot at the creature and it fled.

1909

Long Island communities of Patchogue, Quogue, Eastport, and Westhampton: Residents of these towns reported seeing a "baboon" or "monkey-like" creature on numerous occasions. The creature allegedly emitted a "blood-curdling shriek."

1922

Babylon: Armed police and civilians searched for a "baboon" or "gorilla" after several residents had sightings of such a creature. Nothing was found.

1931

Mineola: A large, hairy, apelike creature startled several witnesses near a Long Island nursery.

Huntington: A "gorilla-like" creature was sighted by a nurseryman and his family as it was crashing through the brush.

Huntington: A farmer reported seeing a "strange animal" near an area where tracks were later found.

Amityville: An eight-foot-tall "gorilla with glowing red eyes" was sighted by several witnesses on various occasions.

1932
Blue Mountain Lake: There were several well-known Adirondack "wild man" sightings. A posse later tracked and shot and killed the "wild man," which turned out to be an African American hermit wearing thick layers of animal skins.

1934
Massapequa: Not far from Amityville, several witnesses reported seeing a "man, beast or demon" roaming throughout Nassau County. One theory was that it was an escaped chimpanzee from nearby Farmingdale, but that theory was discredited by the police.
Amityville: A "mysterious ape-like" creature wreaked havoc on a garage. During the following night, "most of the male residents of the neighborhood (were) sitting on their porches waiting for the animal with shotguns." Nothing more was seen of it, however.

1950
Greene County: Philip Winegard observed a "monkey-like" creature about the size of a ten-year-old boy as it "rose up out of the swamp and grabbed a bird in its hands."
Rouses Point: A family camping reported an apelike creature crossing a road.

1959
Whitehall: Farmer Harry Diekel's neighbor told him that he had seen a "bear-like" creature walking on two legs.

1960

Lewiston: Reports of an apelike creature began circulating in this western New York community.

1965

Sherman: White-haired "swamp monsters" standing twelve to eighteen feet tall were reported by one family on several occasions between 1965 and 1966.

1966

Huntington: Several reports describing a seven-foot-tall humanoid "monster" came from couples who had parked in the Mount Misery area.

1967

Ithaca: During a UFO flap in the area, several reports were made by witnesses who claimed to have seen bigfoot-like creatures in the woods. One boy claimed that one of these creatures tore his jacket.

1974

Richmondtown: Two young boys were terrified by a large, black "furry thing" while they were playing behind the St. Andrew's Episcopal Church parking lot.

1975

Richmondtown: A nurse driving on Richmond Road observed a black hairy figure cross the road on two legs. Ten-inch-long, four-toed footprints were found nearby.

Watertown: A five-foot-tall, two-legged creature "swinging its arms" was observed by Steve Rich, Jerry Emerson, and one other boy while they were walking on State Street Hill.

Whitehall: Clifford Sparks, owner of the Skeene Valley Country Club, encountered an eight-foot-tall "sloth-like" creature near the first green of his golf course. It ran off into the darkness.

Highgate Springs: A man, his son, and his brother observed a large bipedal creature walking "at a casual pace" across a tractor trail in a field.

Whitehall: Police sergeant Wilfred Gosselin and his brother Russell heard an eerie, high-pitched scream that lasted for more than a minute when they were hunting at the intersection of Abair Road and Route 22A.

Saranac Lake: Two men saw a bigfoot squatting by the road near Route 3. They stopped to approach it, but it hurriedly walked away.

1976

Watertown: Two boys reported seeing an eight-foot-tall bigfoot covered with dark hair. Fifteen-inch tracks were found nearby.

Watertown: Two teenage boys saw a hulking, hairy bipedal creature in the woods.

Whitehall: Martin Paddock, Paul Gosselin, and Bart Kinney reported seeing a seven- to eight-foot-tall brown-colored, hairy, two-legged creature in a field off Abair Road. Whitehall Police sergeant Wilfred Gosselin investigated and saw "an awful[ly] tall shadow."

Whitehall: Farmer Harry Diekel found "big human footprints" in a field near the intersection of Abair Road and Route 22A.

Whitehall: Police officer Brian Gosselin and a New York state trooper saw a large, two-legged creature near Abair Road. The beast came within thirty feet of Gosselin's police vehicle. The creature, which Gosselin described as between seven and eight feet tall, had "big red eyes that blurbed about half an inch off its face, no ears, no tail, dark brown hair, almost black; the arms swung down past his knees." The state trooper shone a flashlight in the creature's eyes, whereupon it screamed and ran off.

Hampton: A Whitehall school official observed a large, hairy bipedal creature walk out of Bixby's Apple Orchard and cross the road in front of his car.

Whitehall: A sheriff's deputy and a state trooper found and made plaster casts of nineteen-inch footprints near the Poultney River Bridge in the area of East Bay.

Whitehall: A state trooper observed a large, hairy, two-legged creature in a field off Abair Road.

Lewiston: Police officer Peter Filicetti and his mother reported seeing a bigfoot in a cornfield. Footprints were later found.

Oxbow: A raccoon hunter saw a seven-foot-tall hairy bipedal creature in the woods.

1977

Whitehall: Royal Bennett and his granddaughter Shannon observed what they thought was a "stump" suddenly stand up in a field off Fish Hill Road. They realized what they were seeing was a "honey-colored creature" that they estimated to be seven to eight feet tall and weighing around five hundred pounds. Investigator Bill Brann found a thirteen-and-a-half inch track in the field.

Near Saratoga Springs: A family found fourteen-by-six-inch footprints while camping near Big Eddy.

Theresa: Two pairs of railroad workers reported separate sightings of a large, hairy bipedal creature. Footprints were found at both sites.

1978

Whitehall: A man and his dog were terrified by "inhuman" screams outside the man's house on Abair Road.

Kinderhook: Martha Hallenbeck observed a "big, black hairy thing all curled up" on her lawn.

1979

Whitehall: A man and several members of his family observed a hairy, manlike head peering at them over some bushes near the woods. The man yelled at the creature and it ran off with an "inhuman gait." A week later, the man and the same family members experienced a similar incident while fishing at East Bay River.

Kinderhook: Barry Knights was trapping near Cushing's Hill when he saw "four great big furry things" cross a creek.

Whitehall: Mr. "B" and a friend observed a large bipedal creature walk over a fence in one stride.

Saratoga Lake: A sheriff's deputy investigated a report of strange screams near a trailer park. He found that a tree had been ripped out of the ground and thrown against a trailer.

1980

Kinderhook: "Barbara" observed a seven-and-a-half-foot-tall, two-legged creature with reddish-brown fur cross the road in front of her car and walk into a cornfield. She described it as looking like "a highly evolved ape."

Lawrenceburg: Fred Renaudo observed a bigfoot near his campsite that he said was "breathing real hard, like it had asthma." Fifteen-inch tracks were later found.

Kinderhook: Martha Hallenbeck, Barry Knights, Barbara Knights, and her daughter Chari and granddaughter Melanie were terrorized by a two-legged, hairy creature that screamed and moaned outside Martha's home. Barry fired two shots at it and it ran away into the woods screaming.

Kinderhook: Barry Knights and his cousin Russell Zbierski heard screams while walking at night on Novak Road, near Cushing's Hill. They also saw five hulking figures with "cone-shaped heads" converging in the road in front of them. A female witness who lived on Novak Road saw a large, hairy creature take food from her family's trash can around the same time. Her dog went "crazy" and ran around in circles.

1981

Adirondack Park Region: A cross-country skier found human-like footprints with unusually long strides in the snow.

Indian Lake: A hunter followed eighteen-inch human-like footprints for around one mile. They ended on a ledge, near where an unusual cone-shaped hut was found.

Kinderhook: Strange ten-inch, three-toed tracks were found in a snow-covered field.

Kinderhook: A woman bicycling on Novak Road was startled by a large, hairy bipedal creature that lumbered across the road and into a cornfield.

Kinderhook: Barry Knights and several other campers observed a tall two-legged creature with long arms and no neck that was walking in the area of Cushing's Hill. One of the campers saw "two glowing red eyes" several feet above the ground.

Kinderhook: Strange three-toed tracks that were fourteen inches long and seven inches wide were found by the author.

Greenville: Several reports of a bigfoot-type creature were made by a family living near the woods in this Greene County hamlet. They described multiple encounters with hairy bipedal creatures and found sixteen-inch tracks.

Kinderhook: A rabbit hunter found large humanoid footprints near the Kline Kill Creek.

Kinderhook: Chari Van Allen saw a "big two-legged thing, reddish-brown, which then ran off into the woods."

Davenport: Two children who were fishing were terrified by a bigfoot-like creature that screamed, "gave off a bad smell," and ran away.

1982

Whitehall: Two police officers saw a hairy two-legged creature cross the road near a Washington County Highway Department garage.

Austerlitz: A hunter was startled by an eight-foot tall, red-haired bipedal creature.

Kinderhook: Michael Maab was fishing near a dam when he observed an eight-foot tall, reddish-brown bigfoot-type creature watching him from across the stream, about twenty yards away. Maab described it as having "beady eyes and black fingernails." After two minutes or so of the two of them staring at each other, the creature walked off into the woods.

Kinderhook: The author's father saw a large, black, hairy creature "standing out under a big tree in the yard."

Kinderhook: Several reports of a "white bigfoot" near orchards were made.

Chatham: Reports of a "white bigfoot" were also made in this town, six miles from Kinderhook.

1983

Dexter: A hairy, seven-foot-tall creature was reported near a hardware store.

Kinderhook: A large, black, "bear-like" animal walked on two legs in front of a resident's car on Novak Road. It ambled off into the woods near Cushing's Hill.

Indian Lake: Richard Newman and his son Eric heard something large crashing through the woods near where they were fishing and saw "two large hairy legs" pass by them.

Lake George: Three men on bicycles were traveling on a bike trail when they heard inhuman screams and saw "big red eyes seven feet off the ground" in the nearby woods.

Whitehall: William "Bud" Manell found odd footprints in the snow near the Whitehall dump in East Bay. There were "very long strides" between the tracks.

Stephentown: A large bipedal creature was spotted near Eagle Bridge.

Kinderhook: Joyce Gifford and her daughter were making a right-hand turn near a cow pasture on Route 203 when they saw a seven-foot-tall "hairy man-like creature" standing up from what appeared to be a crouching position. When Gifford stopped the car, the creature glanced their way and then took off in the opposite direction through the cow pasture. Gifford described the creature as having "light brown" hair, which "covered his face except for his eyes and mouth."

1984

Kinderhook: Large humanoid tracks, the biggest at thirteen and three-quarter inches, were found by the Kline Kill Bridge.

Whitehall: A series of bizarre "laughing screams" were heard in several locations at night.

Whitehall: A man saw a huge, hairy ape-like creature in a field.

Whitehall: A seven- to eight-foot-tall hairy creature was seen by several residents.

1985

Whitehall: A woman found large footprints in the snow near her Fourth Avenue home. The bipedal tracks appeared to originate near a treeline and circled her house.

Kinderhook: Margaret Mayer was driving on Route 203 when she saw a six- to seven-foot-tall "bizarre creature" with yellow eyes that was covered with "light-colored fur or feathers."

Kinderhook: Martha Hallenbeck saw round, white "eyes" seven and a half feet off the ground near her back porch at night. "I've never seen anything so bright white," she later said.

1988

Kinderhook: Susan Hallenbeck, a teacher at Ichabod Crane Middle School, was walking in the woods near Cushing's Hill when she heard strange vocalizations that she compared to the sounds that gorillas made in the movie *Gorillas in the Mist*.

1989

Poestenkill: A couple from nearby Averill Park observed a "large, upright figure . . . tall and reddish-blond in color and running very quickly."

Hampton: A teenage boy saw a seven-foot-tall creature that "peeked" at him as he walked along the road.

Hampton: Two teenagers camping saw a "six-foot creature with glowing red eyes" circle their tent.

1990

Ghent: Huge bipedal tracks measuring more than twenty inches long were found in the snow by a farmer. A few days later, similar tracks that trailed off into a thicket were found in the snow in the same area.

Whitehall: A "tall, big, dark" creature was observed crossing a field off a county road.

1991

Loon Lake: Herbert Francisco found huge humanoid tracks, eighteen to twenty-two inches long with ten-foot strides.

Long Lake: Katherine Kaifer reported the sighting of a bigfoot in a wooded area.

2003

Comstock: While driving along Route 22A, Larry Paap observed a creature about four feet high "squatting" in a field. Paap said that it had "shoulder blades seeming pretty massive" and that "its arms were perched." The creature disappeared after staring at Paap for about five seconds. Paap said, "I couldn't figure out how it vanished."

Whitehall: A couple on South Road reported that they heard an "angry" vocalization outside their home and that they caught a glimpse of a four- to five-foot-tall creature.

2004

Clemons: Two Chinese restaurant employees were fishing near a tavern when they observed a "big, tall and skinny" creature "standing" in about five feet of water. One of the witnesses said it looked like an orangutan with a "flat face." The two men watched as the "brown and red" creature waded through the water and disappeared out of sight.

2006

Whitehall: A man told Paul Bartholomew that he had seen a large creature standing near a waste treatment plant near South Bay. The man noted that the creature was "reaching for something . . . (had) long arms, real sharp angles . . . was black, all black . . . shoulders were straight like a linebacker's . . . and a big bull neck . . . He had to be close to seven foot."

Whitehall: "Four very credible professional workers" reported a creature standing near Route Four. One witness said, "It had a white face and black hair and stood about seven feet tall." The driver and his three passengers all saw the creature and drew "very similar" drawings of it.

2008

Whitehall: A fifteen-year-old girl saw a tall creature with "thick, long hair . . . dark brownish color" standing on the edge of the woods near Upper Turnpike Road. She estimated that it was "between seven and eight feet tall." A few moments after the sighting, the girl and her mother heard a "high-pitched screech."

Whitehall: A man was driving his daughter to school when they both observed a humanoid creature cross the road in front of the car. It leapt from a rocky area and the daughter said it turned its head toward them as it ran on two legs across the road and over an embankment.

BIBLIOGRAPY

Bartholomew, Paul, Robert Bartholomew, William Brann, and Bruce Hallenbeck. *Monsters of the Northwoods.* Utica, NY: North Country Books, 1992.

Bartholomew, Robert E. *The Untold Story of Champ: A Social History of America's Loch Ness Monster.* New York: Excelsior/State University of New York Press, 2012.

Bartholomew, Robert E., and Paul B. Bartholomew. *Bigfoot Encounters in New York and New England.* Surrey, BC: Hancock House, 2008.

Carroll, Michael C. *Lab 257: The Disturbing Story of the Government's Secret Germ Laboratory.* New York: William Morrow, 2005.

Coleman, Loren. *Mysterious America.* Revised edition. New York: Paraview Press, 2001.

Crystall, Ellen. *Silent Invasion: The Shocking Discoveries of a UFO Researcher.* New York: St. Martin's Press, 1996.

Gethard, Chris, Mark Moran, and Mark Sceurman. *Weird New York: Your Travel Guide to New York's Local Legends and Best-Kept Secrets.* New York: Sterling, 2005.

Hynek, J. Allen, Philip J. Imbrogno, and Bob Pratt. *Night Siege: The Hudson Valley UFO Sightings.* Second edition. St. Paul, MN: Llewellyn Publications, 1998.

Keel, John A. *The Complete Guide to Mysterious Beings.* New York: Tor Books, 2002.

Streiber, Whitley. *Communion: A True Story.* Revised edition. New York: Avon, 1988.

Zarzynski, Joseph W. *Champ: Beyond the Legend.* Bannister Publications: Chesterfield, Derbyshire, UK: 1984.

ACKNOWLEDGMENTS

The author would like to thank the following individuals and organizations for their invaluable assistance and research: Paul Bartholomew, Robert E. Bartholomew, William Brann, Loren Coleman, the late Dr. Warren L. Cook, Barry Knights, Scott Mardis, The New York State Library, Nick Redfern, Carol Reid, and Joseph W. Zarzynski. I extend a special thanks to my kind and patient editors at Stackpole Books, Kyle Weaver and Brett Keener.